ADIEU, DORDOGNE

ADIEU, DORDOGNE

Roger Kohn

JANUS PUBLISHING COMPANY
London, England

First Published in Great Britain 2007
by Janus Publishing Company Ltd,
105-107 Gloucester Place,
London W1U 6BY

www.januspublishing.co.uk

British Library Cataloguing-in-Publication Data.
A catalogue record for this book is available from the British Library.

ISBN 978-1-85756-608-6

Cover Design: Janus Publishing

Printed by Chris Fowler International Ltd, London

Preface

The dream is always the same. You are sitting on the terrace in the cool of the evening, sipping a glass of chilled white wine, looking out over the garden of your own part of France. Later in the evening you may go down the road to the charming bistro in the village, where the food is cheap and perfect, the service warm and welcoming. Or you may stay at home and have a barbecue, with friends who can speak English popping round to join you. Everything is wonderful. The sun always shines. The roof never leaks.

But the reality can be different. Having owned a house in France for more than thirty years, I think I can speak with some authority on the subject. By and large they were thirty years of pleasure and I don't regret them at all. But the time has come to move on.

This book tries to show what you might encounter if you, too, want to live the dream.

Chapter 1

Getting Started

Le Jarripigier is so small that it doesn't really deserve to be on the map, but it is. If you get a Michelin map 75 and find the N89 road, which runs from Perigueux to Brive and beyond, you will find the town of Thenon. Go two kilometres south, along the road to Rouffignac and you will find the village of Le Jarripigier.

The core of the hamlet (it isn't really a village at all) consists of a handful of houses and barns, most of them empty and crumbling away because nobody wants them. The only modern house (by which I mean a house that was built after World War II) is on the right-hand side as you go from Thenon. It is owned by the Dartinset family. Just beyond their house is an empty building whose roof has been slowly collapsing for the last decade or so (it is now being fitfully restored) and next to that is the home of Jean-Paul Dartinset (son of the other Dartinsets) and his family. There are more abandoned buildings beyond that.

On the other side of the road are two houses. Ours was the first one you come to and beyond that is another property that is owned by the Smiths of Leicester. So two of the occupied houses in Le Jarripigier are owned by foreigners. The locals don't seem to mind. When I bought my first house in the Dordogne, more than thirty years ago, the former owner was asked what she felt about selling her house to an Englishman. She answered: "It could have been worse. It could have gone to a Parisian."

One reason for this might be that for centuries Britain (or at least England) and southwestern France were united under a common monarch. This is thanks to Eleanor of Aquitaine, who married Henry II of England and produced such paragons as Richard the Lionheart and King John. The northern French were foreign to both. A few years ago my wife Heather and I went to Castillon la Bataille, a small town on the River Dordogne on the way to Bordeaux. Its claim to

1

fame is that it is there, in 1453, that the last battle of the Hundred Years' War was fought. This historic event, which was a French victory, is now used as an excuse for a splendid pageant that takes place in July, features a cast of several hundred people and brings a huge number of tourists to the area. We were told about it by some French friends in Bordeaux and we went expecting an interesting evening telling how the noble French drove out the wicked invaders. Not at all. The people of Castillon and England were on the same side during the war.

Bordeaux and Aquitaine had already been occupied by the French, who treated the locals terribly, by making them pay taxes and so on. In their despair the Bordelais called on their old allies, the English, to come to their rescue. And so an English army, which by rights should have been back at home preparing for the Wars of the Roses (which followed a few years later) and led by the Earl of Shrewsbury (a veteran of Agincourt) sailed off to save them. The French retreated and Shrewsbury, who is usually known in France by his family name of Talbot, moved inland. At Castillon the French prepared for battle. All went well for Talbot until the Bretons switched sides and joined the French. The result was a defeat and death for Talbot and Castillon and Bordeaux once again came under the yoke of the French (or Parisians). The story had a happy ending because eventually the Parisians allowed the Bordelais to export their wine to England and prosperity returned.

The pageant took place on a hill outside Castillon. The real battle took place near the river, but the site is now occupied by farmland, so the re-enactment had to be shifted. There is a monument to Talbot on the site of the battle itself, erected by local French admirers. Whatever the rights and wrongs of the issue, the pageant was a splendid affair. Talbot charged around the hillside on a white horse and fell nobly at the end, overwhelmed by odds and treachery. The spectacle was terrific, the music and sound effects impressive. It was worth losing a battle for, especially as we still get their wine.

But the reason why the people of southwest France tolerate foreigners is more prosaic than historical and has to do with money. The fact is that without the British, Dutch and some other foreigners (including, of course, Parisians) the whole of the countryside of this beautiful part of France would be full of abandoned, unwanted houses. *Maisons secondaires* might not be the ideal solution to rural depopulation, but they are better than ruins and, what is more, the people who own them do provide an income for the area and jobs for local builders and craftsmen.

So, generally speaking, the local people are glad to see us. They are flattered that we like their area so much. They are happy to be friends. The trouble is that most of them can't speak anything but French and the British can't speak anything but English. My advice to anyone wanting to go on holiday in the Dordogne or especially to anyone who wants to buy a property there is to learn French before you go. It's their country, after all. Why should they learn your language?

My first house was in Sergeac, a small village on the River Vézère, about ten kilometres from Le Jarripigier and close to the thriving town of Montignac. In the summer Montignac is full of life and people, mainly because it has a famous cave, Lascaux. Sergeac is also quite prosperous and we liked it because lots of people lived there and others had holiday homes there. We liked chatting to people on our way to the rubbish bin and playing *pétanque* in the afternoons. Anyone who happened to be passing by would be invited to play. It didn't really matter whether you could play or not and women were just as welcome as men.

The trouble with Sergeac was that our house was small and didn't have much of a garden so in the summer the heat was intense and it was difficult to escape. We decided that we wanted something bigger and in 1988 we sold the house to my cousin and started looking around.

We took our time. We looked at houses further south, including some on the other side of the Dordogne, but for some reason the estate agents all thought we wanted something remote. We went down long tracks through the woods and investigated partly restored castles. None of them was suitable, because we didn't want to be remote and we didn't want lots of work to do when we found somewhere. We looked around Montignac and came close to buying a house at Muguets, just north of the N89 near La Mule Blanche. But in the end we chose the house at Le Jarripigier. It was a big house and had lots of land, most of it wooded. There were people nearby and Thenon was not too far away. We also liked the owners, Roger and Pauline Brière, who were planning to buy a house in Thenon itself, which would be more convenient for them (he is an architect and she worked at the post office).

By 1990 the house was ours. My wife Heather and I were able to buy the house because she had sold her own home in Rochester, Kent, and I had sold the house at Sergeac. This gave us enough money to buy the house at Le Jarripigier and still have enough left over for furniture and, most important of all, a swimming pool.

Chapter 2

Buying a House in France

This is not intended to be a comprehensive guide to buying a property in France. There are plenty of books available that set out to do just that. This chapter simply contains a few observations that might come in useful.

My first advice is don't – unless...

I, of course, ignored that advice myself. It all seemed so easy back in 1972. Property was cheap and so were dreams. To some extent they still are, so I expect that for many people the dream will be irresistible. They'll go ahead no matter what anyone says.

So my second piece of advice is do not let the dream become a nightmare. This sounds sensible enough, but it is easy to go just that little bit too far. Unless you love DIY and know what you are doing and/or have lots of money, do not consider converting a ruin into a luxury villa. The moment the cost of your holiday house starts to affect your quality of life back home the dream will start to fade and the nightmare will begin. I have put this advice high on my list and perhaps it should be right at the top.

Closely allied to the above is piece of advice number three: decide what you want the house for. Are you planning to move there permanently? Do you want it for holidays? If so, when do you plan to go there – summer, winter, autumn, spring – or any time you feel like going?

Having decided that, agree on what sort of house you want. In the country or in a town? Isolated or in a village? How many rooms? How much land do you need? All of this will depend on factors such as: do you have any children? How old are they? Will they be interested in going to France in five years' time? Should the house be modern or old?

These questions seem obvious, I know, but they are absolutely crucial. I believe that most people (I include myself back in 1972) think that a house in France will be all pleasure. We picture ourselves, as I said before, sitting on the terrace in the evening sunshine, sipping a glass of chilled local wine before going down to the restaurant for a thrilling meal at a ridiculously low price. This is the life, we tell ourselves fondly, this is what it's all about. But it isn't.

Houses in France, like houses in Britain or indeed any other country, are usually about money. Roofs need replacing. The heating goes wrong. The walls need papering. Do you want to spend your two-week holiday standing on a ladder with a paintbrush in your hand? If the answer is no, think about staying in a hotel.

It is possible to make money out of your house, by renting it to other people. But it is not a guaranteed way of covering your costs. Most people want to go on holiday in the summer and those who have children want to go during the school holidays. That generally means August, probably the time you want to go yourselves. People looking for a *gite* want certain things. They want space for the family and a reasonable amount of comfort. They want everything to be arranged when they get there. They don't want things to go wrong. Nowadays they usually want a swimming pool. I suggest you look at the Internet or holiday brochures to see the sort of thing that is available and is required. You will learn that a house with a pool and accommodation for eight people can earn well over £1,000 a week in August, but before you pocket the cash there are a number of expenses.

You first have to find someone who wants to rent a house. That could mean advertising, or finding a company that can handle the deal for you. They will expect a substantial commission. You will have to find someone who can get the house ready for the new arrivals: that means cleaning the house when the last tenants have gone, changing the sheets, mowing the lawn etc. They will all need paying. Then there is tax. When the French tax people learn that you are renting a house in their country they will expect you to pay them a slice of the profit. The same is true of the tax people in Britain. The more commercial you are, the more money you will make – but the more you have to spend. And there is always the danger of something going wrong. You will, after all, probably be renting your house to strangers. There is no guarantee that they will look after your dream. They may leave it in a mess or run off with your pots and pans or break the vacuum cleaner. The fortune you are banking on earning in August is beginning to slide away – and don't forget that August is exceptional. The holiday season is very short – June, July and August. People won't be begging for accommodation in November. And if you rent your house in the high season you won't be able to go there yourself. If you do, remember that you won't be making any money during that time. Your lovely August break could in effect cost you £4,000 or so.

Of course, if you have enough money (which you should do, before you even start thinking about buying a house) you could pay somebody to do the work for you. But who? The chances are you won't know the area, and above all you won't know the people. So do make the effort to learn the language before you even knock on the estate agent's door. This is important, especially if you want to buy a property. The estate agent might speak English, but most other people will not. And if you can't speak their language there is a possibility that you might get ripped off. I say there is a possibility. That is about all. The French are just as honest as we are (which is another way of saying that they are just as dishonest). I have dealt with numerous builders, decorators, painters, gardeners and so on over the years and I can say that only once have I been disappointed. Most of the people who have worked for us have been honest, competent, reliable and a pleasure to deal with.

There are various ways of meeting these paragons. One is to ask the estate agent. This is not always the best way. You might be buying a house in an area with which he is not intimately acquainted. He might have a brother in law who needs a job. He might have an arrangement with a local company, which pays him 10% for every introduction.

You could go to the local Syndicat d'Initiatif. Most towns have them. They are information offices and tourist offices combined. They might not recommend an individual carpenter – that would be unfair on the others – but they will probably be able to give you a list. The best way to get to know artisans and workmen is to ask your neighbours. In fact, getting to know your neighbours is essential for peace of mind. In our experience, French people are friendly and they have always been glad to provide help. If they suggest a carpenter it usually means that the carpenter has a good reputation in the area. Your neighbours wouldn't recommend someone who was no good, because it would reflect badly on them. Also encourage your neighbours to keep an eye on your property when you are not there. They will probably do it any way (nosey neighbours are very good), but they will like to think that you trust them and it is also useful to find someone you can leave a key with. If the plumber has to repair a leak in the middle of winter when you are not there, the neighbours can let him have the key to your house (and also keep an eye on him while he is working).

Quite apart from costs of carpenters, plumbers, electricians and other artisans, you will face certain regular costs, which cannot really be avoided. Here are some of the bills I received in one year (the figures are in euros):

Swimming pool (opening it in the summer and closing it in the autumn)	520.00
EDF/GDF (electricity)	500.00
Telephone	473.00
Total gas (for heating and cooking)	845.00
Local rates	492.00
Garbage collection	130.00
Water	107.00
Property taxes	624.00
Total	3,691.00

It is a good idea, before you buy your dream house, to visit the area several times before making a choice. At least one of these visits should be out of season. Because France is south of Britain it is generally warmer, but some parts are higher and further away from the mild protection of the sea. They can be cold and they also get quite a lot of rain. It is lovely sitting by the pool. But it is not much fun sitting indoors watching the rain streaming down the windows and wondering what's on the telly back home. Out of season things tend to close down, especially in the country. Some restaurants will shut. So will castles, gardens, museums and other tourist spots. It will be too cold for swimming and anyway the pool will be clogging up with leaves. Do you still want to live there?

I can remember when I bought my first house in France. I did it with my mother, who had read some articles about how cheap property was and how wonderful France was and so we flew off to Bordeaux and hired a car. We had arranged some meetings with estate agents (all English or English speaking) and we spent several days looking at empty houses, mostly ruined, in the Dordogne. Eventually we found the house in Sergeac and bought it because it was cheap and we liked the village. I remember that it cost about £1,900 and needed a lot of work, including mending a crack in the wall.

The builder we picked (recommended by the estate agent) was less than perfect. We worked out the repair costs on the back of an envelope (we estimated what we could afford and then adjusted the costs accordingly: not the best way of doing things). Years later the work was still not finished. The builder told us that to repair the crack he would have to replace the roof, which was made from lauzes, very heavy slabs of limestone, which are used on roofs in the Dordogne area and have to be installed by specialist craftsmen. Our builder hired two lads from Yorkshire who needed the work. The next winter we watched the rain first trickling, then pouring through the gaps between the stones. The whole job had to be done again. The whole episode amounts to a classic example of how not to buy and renovate a property in a foreign country.

So, in addition to the other advice given above, I suggest that before buying a property that is ripe for conversion or in need of repair (estate agents in France use the same jargon as they do here) know what you are doing. If you don't, find somebody who does, and if that isn't possible either, have enough money available to pay somebody who does. Work out your costs very carefully and then double them, because there are bound to be extras that you did not anticipate.

It is not customary in rural France to have a survey done when you are buying a house. You go to look at a house and, if you like it, you buy it. That is one reason why it is best to look at houses when it is raining – it stops you getting carried away by the sunshine. You can usually spot if the roof is sound, if there is woodworm or if the location is right. But check to see if the house has water laid on and if electricity is available. It is surprising how many don't.

All of this sounds pessimistic. I prefer to call it realistic. Buying your house in Britain will probably be your biggest ever expense and naturally, you take it seriously. Buying a house abroad will probably be your next biggest expense, so treat that seriously as well. Some people simply do not think things through properly. I knew some people who decided to buy a farm in France because the land there was so much cheaper than it was in southern England. They didn't stop to consider why it was cheaper. They simply thought that although the land was cheaper the prices they could get for their produce would be the same as they could obtain back home. They weren't. I knew some other people who moved to France and bought a large property, which they thought they would be able to fill with paying guests. They did – but only for two months in the summer. Many people seem to think that they can earn a good living by giving English lessons. The fact that there might not be any people in the area who want to learn English and the equally important fact that the would-be teacher has no qualifications or experience of teaching is ignored.

On the other hand, I know other people for whom everything has gone even better than they dreamt. One couple bought a holiday home and they were delighted when the local schoolmaster came to their door and asked if they would like to send their children to the local school when they were in France. This would help them learn French and they might even enjoy it, which they did. The children were soon bi-lingual and the parents made lots of French friends, proving that the best way of getting to know people is to have children, or perhaps a dog.

The local tree surgeon in our area is British – even the French use him, because he is good and he speaks the language. Dutch people run one of the most successful campsites near us. Other ex-patriates have become successful estate agents, journalist, winegrowers and business people.

Chapter 3

Sergeac

As I said, it was my mother's idea to buy a house in France. She had read various articles in the newspapers about the southwest of France, the part the French call Périgord and the English generally refer to as the Dordogne. Property was cheap, the articles proclaimed. You could buy your patch of paradise for a song.

My father was not interested in a house in France, but I thought it sounded quite a good idea. We went to see the secretary of our local building society (who had my mortgage) and he thought buying a house in France was a splendid idea. Yes, he would increase my mortgage.

So, one day in the autumn of 1972, we flew off to Bordeaux, hired a car, and headed east to the Promised Land. We were armed with a list of estate agents, helpfully provided by the newspaper articles, and we had arranged to see them all. The first were in Riberac, in the west of the department of Dordogne. Even then it was popular with the British and the estate agent, who had lived in England for many years, spoke fluent English. This was a help, as my French was on the primitive side. He showed us a house in a village to the west of the town. It had no water and was not connected to electricity either, but the estate agent assured us that this would not be a problem. Back in his office we sat at his desk and he held out a pen towards us. All we had to do was sign. I thought hard and said to my mother that I thought we should go for a little walk first. We decided that it would be foolish to buy the first house we had seen. We didn't know the area, and there were lots of other places to see. If we still liked the house near Riberac, well, we could call back again. It would probably still be available, although the estate agent had tried to persuade us that people were queuing up to buy it. We went back to the estate agent's office. He looked at us gravely and said we were making a big mistake.

We continued eastwards and saw lots of houses. We came to the conclusion that the estate agent was probably right. We had made a mistake. One problem was that the houses we liked were too expensive and the ones that we could afford we didn't like. French inheritance laws increased our difficulty. They insist on looking after the interests of the children. When someone dies the children are entitled to a fair share of the estate. Primogeniture does not exist in France. In Britain we are used to the system where the parent can leave everything to the eldest son, daughter, widow or the local cats' home. You can't do that in France. And so many of the properties we saw were divided up in a most peculiar way. We would be told: "The left half of the house and that barn over there, together with two fields half a mile away go with the property. But the rest belongs to someone else."

Finally, we arrived at Les Eyzies, which is situated on the River Vézère and is regarded as the capital of prehistory, because so many archaeological discoveries have been made in the area. We stayed at the Hotel du Centre, which is still there, although the name has changed. It was very comfortable but what impressed us most was the fact that we had fresh strawberries for dinner. In those days it was virtually impossible to get fresh strawberries in England unless tennis was being played at Wimbledon. That meal was almost as memorable as one we had at our hotel in Riberac, where the owner served us home-made pâté, from a large jam jar, using a long spoon.

We looked at more houses and liked some of them, but they were too expensive. Finally, the estate agents, who were English, suggested that we might like to look at a house in a village called Sergeac. Sergeac is on the River Vézère , a few miles west of Montignac, which was then a small market town known only because it is near the prehistoric cave paintings of Lascaux, which have been described by one expert as the "Sistine Chapel of prehistory". The house there was small, in need of total repair, but was cheap. We rather liked it. We especially liked the village, which was quite small and compact, but seemed to be very friendly and charming and it even had a restaurant, which was listed in the Michelin guide. The price was 16,000 francs, about £1,900.

The estate agents assured us that it would be quite a simple job to make the house habitable, an ideal summer home. They knew builders, carpenters and others who could do the necessary work for us. It wouldn't cost very much. So we signed on the dotted line. The estate agents were working in collaboration with a French estate agent from Les Eyzies and he handled most of the negotiation with the owner, a widow who had used the house not as a home but as a shed for drying tobacco. He took his wife with him, because the owner spoke with such a strong local patois that he couldn't understand her. His wife came from the area and could.

By early 1973 the legal and financial details had been settled and were now the proud owners of our own chateau in France. The property consisted of a house built on three levels. The main living area consisted of one room at the top of a flight of stone stairs running up from the garden to the front door. It was a large room, about 18 metres long and 12 metres wide. At one end was a precarious flight of steps leading up to the loft. There was also a cellar (or cave in French), which was approached by means of a door leading from the garden. You could not get to it from inside the house. The garden itself was about 20 metres long by 12 metres wide. A gate led to the village square and there were other properties on each side of the house and in front.

It was small, but it did have one rare and fairly unique feature. That was the roof, which was built of lauze. Lauzes are small slabs of limestone, roughly shaped into a rectangle, which were a traditional roofing material in the Périgord region of France. Instead of being laid parallel with the slope of the roof, like tiles and slates, they are laid horizontally, forming layers that slope back gradually following the angle of the roof. The layer of stones that results is very thick and exerts a tremendous pressure on the roof timbers and on the walls of the house. I was told that one square metre of lauze in the Dordogne could weight up to 90 kilos, while further south they could weigh 120 kilos a square metre. Lauzes themselves are nowadays very rare, partly because they are expensive and partly because building a lauze roof is a highly specialised job that ordinary roofers cannot do.

We ignored the disadvantages and thought only of the advantages. We had our own house in France, our own cottage where we would be able to spend idyllic free holidays sipping wine, eating the delicious local food and lazing in the sun.

The reality was a little different, and not nearly so idyllic. The problems were caused by the builder recommended to us. I wouldn't say he was a crook, but if someone else did I wouldn't spring to his defence. I don't know what the French for "rip-off" is, but somehow the phrase springs to mind whenever I think of him. Years later I heard that he had gone bankrupt. I felt sorry for the men who had worked for him and lost their jobs as a result, but I didn't shed a tear for him. What made the whole episode even more annoying was the fact that all the other people who have worked for us – and there have been quite a few over the years – proved to be honest, reliable, efficient and good at their jobs.

The secret to hiring craftsmen and workmen is to ask your neighbours. They will usually be happy to help and the people they recommend will be anxious to justify their confidence. The trouble is that when you are buying a house for the first time you don't know the neighbours.

When we bought the house the agents gave us a rough idea of how much we would have to spend to make it habitable. The estimate turned out to be very rough indeed. The first thing that needed to be done was to put in a front door and a window overlooking the tiny garden.

The builder who had been recommended to us came and had a look and then told us that it would be difficult. There was a crack in the wall that was so bad that the wall would have to be rebuilt. That would involve taking off the roof. The whole job, he estimated, would come to more than 36,000 francs (more than twice what we had paid for the property in the first place).

Our builder told us that the crack in the wall had been caused by the weight of the stones. This was an expense that we had not been counting on but we felt obliged to agree. So the lauzes were removed (we never saw them again) and the wall was demolished and rebuilt. Then we had to replace the roof. Because of the expense, we wanted to use tiles instead of lauzes, but the French government Ministry of Beaux-Arts insisted that we used lauzes. This would have cost about four times much, and eventually it was agreed that the first metre would be in lauze and rest in tiles. We were grateful for this, because replacing the lauze just for one metre cost as much as doing the rest of the roof. Not that our builder did much: he recruited two young men from Yorkshire, who were trying to make a new life in France, and gave them the job, lauze and all. The result was that the roof was replaced within budget and leaked like a sieve. This led to a protracted legal battle; the builder denied responsibility and although we eventually got a legal ruling against him he still refused to pay. This would have meant further legal battles, which would have taken years, so we decided to give up and get someone else to do the job. We did this by asking the neighbours and the roofer they recommended turned out to be excellent.

I have copies of the letters and bills received during this period. It lasted about ten years and the correspondence makes depressing reading. It is not just the money involved, but the time we lost. For most of the 1970s the house was virtually uninhabitable: we would go down there in the summer and look at our ruin, rather than live in our chateau. Our builder was not only unreliable financially, he was also slow. We got to know numerous excuses – work had been held up by unseasonable weather, was a favourite.

It turned out that there were all sorts of other things that had to be done, like laying on water and electricity. We had to have a *fosse septique* (septic tank) fitted (cost in 1976, 4,000 francs). A staircase was installed from the ground floor to the first floor and we had a new floor laid down in what became the bedroom. We put in a bathroom.

The work on the wall and roof had resulted in the staircase to the front door being virtually destroyed, so we had to replace that. By the late 1970s the house was at least habitable and during the 1980s we were able to spend some very happy holidays in Sergeac. We liked the house, but we loved the village and we adored the area. On summer evenings we would sit on the terrace by the front door, sipping wine and planning where we would eat; just the way we had done in dreams, back home in England. Sometimes in the afternoon I would go out into the square and play pétanque with a group that included local Sergeacois and people from Marseille and Bordeaux, all attracted to Sergeac, like us, by the relaxed, easy way of life, the friendliness of the people and the chance to relax. We got to know the local people (and the other summer visitors) and in a way became part of the community, just as we had always wanted.

We made further changes to the house. We installed a staircase leading down to the cave and the cave itself was converted into a spare bedroom. But by the 1980s we were becoming aware that the house itself was less than ideal. It was small, for one thing, and the garden was tiny. There was no way of escaping the heat, which in the height of summer can be intense. We dreamt of a garden with grass, trees and even a swimming pool. One day my wife and I decided to go on a sightseeing trip further south, but the temperature soared to 40 degrees and we gave up: it was too hot to drive, too hot to see sights, too hot even to swim. We wanted a breeze, trees and shade. But there was none around. And so we decided to look for another property.

My cousin Brian and his wife Nita had been frequent visitors to the house and did a lot of invaluable DIY work there. They offered to buy the house. That meant that all my wife Heather and I had to do was to find another property. Ideally we would have liked a house in Sergeac, but there were none available. So we began to look elsewhere. Finally, we found a house near Thenon. It was rather north of the area we knew best, but it had a big garden, with room for a swimming pool, and even more enticing, we could move straight in without doing any repair work.

Chapter 4

The House at Le Jarripigier

Having taken possession of the house in 1990, Heather and I started work on converting it into our dream home. Fortunately we could move straight in. One of our rules was that we would not buy a house that needed lots of hard work converting it. We had done that at Sergeac and didn't really want to repeat the experience at Le Jarripigier.

The first few years were interesting and productive. We knew more or less what we wanted – a comfortable house with a garden and room for a swimming pool. We would have liked a house in or close to a village, but that was not possible: Le Jarripigier at that time only contained a handful of houses, most of which were empty and in ruins. Still, in other respects the house was ideal. The garden especially needed quite a lot of work, but that didn't bother us. We both quite liked gardening and watching things grow around us.

The main door to the house led directly into the kitchen/diner, a large room on the ground floor that had a small utility room on the left. On the far side of the room were some steps leading up to a landing, from which doors led to a toilet, a bedroom, the main living room and some stairs leading down to another room (which could have been turned into a bedroom). The living room, a large and elegantly proportioned room, had French windows leading down to the garden and another staircase leading upstairs. At the top was a large bedroom, with timbered ceiling, a bathroom, toilet and another room that was not being used, but which could be converted into a bedroom. Below the living room was a large cellar.

The garden was about 100 metres long and 50 metres wide. About half of it was wooded and was so dense in brambles and nettles as to be almost impenetrable. There was a small, roughly mown lawn and between that and the house was a sort of driveway, mostly covered in weeds. They were quite thick when we bought the house. By the time we arrived for our first stay, a few months after that, the weeds had grown to be higher than the car.

We didn't mind that, though, because we could use the house and the garden could be tackled in time.

We were fortunate in knowing several artisans and workmen from our days in Sergeac. These included a mason, a plumber, a plasterer and several other people who had done excellent work for us before and could, we knew, be trusted. There were certain basic tasks to be carried out: getting connected to the water and electricity services, getting a telephone laid on and so on. Then we went to local furniture shops to buy furniture. I have the bills in front of me as I write this: a wardrobe from Meubles de la Vézère (a shop at Le Bugue that no longer exists), price 1,260 francs; two divan bases, 2,668 francs; and there were quite a lot of others, even though we brought some furniture from Sergeac.

But the main item was the swimming pool. Since one hot summer in Sergeac when we could hardly venture out of doors because of the heat (and couldn't stay indoors because it was even worse there) we had decided that a pool was a priority, not because we loved swimming (I don't very much and Heather can't) but because we could could use it to cool off. There are lots of places – lakes and rivers – where you can go swimming, but you have to go a long way to get there and we wanted something that we could sit beside with our wine and jump into when it got too hot to do that.

There are scores of companies in France that specialise in building swimming pools for holiday homes and several magazines full of glossy photos showing what you can hope to get. We were suitably beguiled, but after looking around for a while we opted for the Jean Desjoyaux company, which had an office at Terrasson, halfway up the N89 between Thenon and Brive. They came and examined the site and by the summer of 1992 we had a swimming pool. It cost about 80,000 francs (digging the hole was extra) and measured 10 by 5 metres – a bit bigger than we needed or really wanted, but we got carried away by the sunshine. When you order a pool that is what you will get – a hole in the ground filled by a concrete frame lined with plastic. Ours also came complete with a filtering/cleaning system, steps and an underwater light, which can be quite useful if you want to go skinny-dipping at midnight.

It was, of course, empty and had to be filled by a hosepipe from a tap outside the kitchen door. That took two or three days. Since water in France is metred this must have cost a fortune, but I don't know how much because I didn't dare look at my water bill. A swimming pool is, from a biological point of view, nothing more than a pond or big puddle. If you want to use it for swimming then you have to make sure that the water is clean. This means making sure that it keeps moving, which in our pool was done through a pump and filter system. You also have to keep an eye on the chemistry of the water: the system we had involved continually checking and, if necessary, adjusting the chlorine and pH levels. It's not very difficult but you have to be there to do it. If you are away you might have to get someone else to keep an eye on it and that someone might require payment – and certainly a supply of chemicals. When ours was installed I received a bill from Desjoyaux for chemical products that were considered necessary for the health of the pool. It came to 939 francs in the summer of 1992. Despite the money we had spent, the pool was still pretty basic; a hole in the ground with steps leading into water. So we got a mason from Sergeac who had done a lot of excellent work for us there to install a paved terrace around the pool. This meant that we didn't have to get into the pool with muddy feet every time we went for a swim, but the main advantage of the terrace was that it was a sitting area, where we could have barbecues and just lop around. If you want to do the same I suggest that you make the terrace as big as possible. Ours has 2 metres on one side and 3 on the other. Remember also, that French law now says that if you have a pool in an unenclosed garden then it must be fenced in. I think this is to stop children falling in, but it can have other advantages. Neighbouring dogs like to visit gardens, especially if the owners are away, and ours has been visited by cattle and, on at least one occasion, by a deer. One of our friends had a pool and put a green winter cover on at the end of the season. A passing horse thought it was a lawn and decided to walk on it. Our friend had to jump into the pool (in November) and comfort the horse until a neighbour arrived with a tractor and was able to get the horse out.

The pool meant that we could loaf around in the sun sipping wine and keeping cool, but we found that this wasn't enough, somehow, so we started on the garden. Basically, this meant hacking back the jungle that should have been a wood. I started at one side and Heather at the other and we began chopping and slashing until we met in the middle, having cleared a path about 3 feet wide. We realised that making the wood useful – this meant having somewhere to hang the hammock in the shade – would take years.

We also decided that we would have to install central heating. People always think of holiday homes as places to go in the summer, but if you want to go out of season you want to be comfortable, which means warm. We had a very good wood fire in the living room and a huge open fire in the kitchen. Some of the rooms also had small electric heaters, which worked quite well but were expensive to run and did not heat the house sufficiently in the winter (or even spring and autumn). It seemed ridiculous to us to have a second home that we could only use in the summer. The whole thing was even sillier because every year we would pay a plumber to empty the pipes and taps. This was necessary to stop them freezing up and bursting in the cold winter months.

As time passed, I also started to keep a diary. I don't keep a diary normally, but so much was happening in France that I thought it might be useful to keep a record. It really began when we took an old computer down to France with us one year. We linked it up to the Internet and, by doing so, were able to keep in touch with people at home, since we could access all emails sent to our home in England. The rest of this book consists of the diary that I began in 1998.

It turned out to be an eventful year.

Chapter 5

Dear Diary

Wednesday, 15 April 1998

We are down here for Easter. The weather has been foul, wet, cold, windy, but it is even worse in England, where some people have been drowned in floods in the Midlands. Here in France there have been a number of fatal accidents on the roads apparently caused by hail. Two nights ago there was a severe frost and this seems to have affected some of the soft fruit at least – the kiwi fruit at Jardiland[1] today were limp and brown-leaved.

Wednesday, 10 June 1998

So much for Easter – I didn't write much, did I?

We came down this time by train, with my mother. Eurostar to Lille and then TGV. It seemed quite a good idea and worked out quite well. The train cost £54 each and then £119 to hire the car (a Peugeot 205 from Europcar) for a week. The Eurostar was fine. We left Ashford at 9.30 and raced to Lille, reaching a maximum of 186mph (300kph) about half an hour after leaving Calais. That was announced with great pride by the train manageress. There were a few Scots on the train, a family – father, mother and two sons – and various others dressed in kilts and flags, all going to the World Cup match with Brazil. Everyone seemed in good humour. At Lille we had to hang about for a while, and because we had booked the tickets at different times one seat was reserved two coaches away from the other two. No real problems, however, I sat where there was a vacant place and every time someone got on I moved.

The train was a TGV but was actually very slow because it kept stopping – at Douai, Arras, CDG Airport, Marne La Vallée for Euro Disney and then other stops, including Poitiers, before we reached Angoulême, where our hire car was waiting. The train was quite crowded – a party of German tourists also got off at Angoulême, as did a young British couple, she complete with *Cosmopolitan* and he with a French phrase book. The weather changed completely during the journey – from cold, cloudy and wet in Ashford, to bright spells and then glorious sunshine.

We didn't eat much – didn't even go to the buffet. The main lesson learned was not to take so much luggage next time – it was difficult negotiating the stairs, with cases full of books, portable computers and so on.

It took much longer from Angoulême than we expected. The car was quite small and had to carry quite a load. The road was narrow and quite busy, so we couldn't go very fast, and then at Perigueux I followed the signs intended to keep lorries out of the town centre. As a result we headed off south and then southwest until we reached the start of the new by-pass round the city and headed northeast. The result was that although we got to Angoulême at 4.50pm and left the town (after a coffee) at 5.30pm we didn't get close to home until 7.30pm. So we decided to go to the Orée du Bois[2] for dinner before going home and we had a very good meal indeed, for 105 francs each. Soup, followed by ham and pâté salad (for me) and cheese and pâté for Mum and Heather. They both had an omelette and I had a confit and by then we were all pretty full, so we missed the cheese and went on to dessert.

We went to bed at about 10pm. We were all tired. We were surprised at how long it took to get to the house from Angoulême.

The next day – the 10th – we lazed around. We got some eggs, milk etc. in Thenon, but several shops were closed, including the hardware shop and the bakers (both of them). Mel[3] had been over and the garden looked lovely. The seringats were blooming and there were nuts on the hazels, but I didn't see any cherries. The pool was crystal clear and about 24 degrees. The water tasted brackish and Heather went in and said it seemed more buoyant than it did before, so all the salt must have had an effect. It certainly seems much clearer and brighter than it did before.[4]

Monday, 15 June 1998

An interesting day or two. On Saturday we stayed in and had a simple meal of cauliflower cheese. It was delicious. Heather put in most of the cheeses that we had left over and the sauce was rich and creamy.

During the night she got up with bad stomach pains and sciatica in the left hip. It was so painful that she couldn't sleep and the next day was in agony. I kept taking up hot water bottles but this didn't do much good. She kept being sick and couldn't face the thought of eating. We began to get worried about whether we would be able to leave on Tuesday and thought we might have to go to the doctor.

By Monday morning she was feeling better – not hungry, but the sciatica had gone and she had stopped being sick. But we are not sure about eating this evening. I booked a table at Chez Maria,[5] but I don't think Heather will go. Mum and I will go and just have a light meal, I think. I did most of the clearing up this morning and some more strimming in the garden. We have to leave tomorrow morning at about 6am to catch the TGV at Angoulême. Everything looks very flourishing; no wonder, because of the rain. But frosts have wiped out much of the blossom, so it looks like no cherries this year. But there are nuts on the hazel tree, which is the first time we have seen them.

Mel came over twice to discuss plans. These mainly involve the room over the kitchen, which will be plastered. The beams will not apparently cause much problem. We also have to have electricity and points put in and we want to get central heating done at the same time. It will be gas central heating, probably from Total. We'll have a tank buried outside the north-facing wall. The earth removed will be put in the ditch by the front of the house. That is where the bath water comes out – we watched it one evening. Mel will put another pipe in to take the overflow down the ditch a little further. Filling in the hole there will improve the appearance of the house and make the access at the front easier. This is intended to be a winter job, so by next spring it should be in very good shape.

Thursday, 9 July 1998

What developments! Our one week holiday has turned into a marathon, because Heather's problems turned out not to be dietary but due to an ovarian cyst, which had become twisted around somehow. The pains began again in earnest the morning we were supposed to leave. We got up early and I went over to the farm and the Dartinsets told me that Doctor Bardet in Rouffignac was the best choice. So we set off there at 8.15am on the Tuesday morning, 16

June. We had to wait for a couple of people who had made appointments and then he saw us. A young man, very pleasant. He prodded around the middle for a few seconds and then announced that there was a severe blockage in the abdomen. "Do you know the way to the hospital in Perigueux?" he asked me. As it happened I did, but he said it would be easier if I just followed the ambulance, which he duly arranged. Then he phoned the hospital emergency department (*Urgences*) and arranged for them to be waiting. The examination cost was 110 francs. The taxi was waiting for us when he finished and off we went.

At the hospital they were waiting. Heather went in for her examination and after an hour or so they came and told me that she would have to stay in for tests and then an operation, which might be on Monday. I rang Mum and then went back to the house. Lots of phone calls followed. We hadn't got our E111s with us, but I phoned the Coutts' hotline and they said they would take care of everything. Fortunately, Heather had her National Health number. I vowed to make a list of everything that we should take in future on holiday – E111, addresses, phone numbers, etc. I called the office and broke the news that I would not be back to work on time.

For the next few days I went in to the hospital each afternoon. It was very comfortable and efficient. Heather had her own room (11508), with television (I paid extra for that) and the nurses came round regularly and the doctors every so often and she was taken off and given X-rays and lots of other tests, far more than I think she would have received at an NHS hospital at home. The first X-ray revealed nothing, but later scans showed that she had a really massive cyst which was beginning to put pressure on other organs, such as the intestines. This, of course, explained many of the problems she had been having over the years, going right back to a visit to Sergeac more than ten years ago, when we had to go to the doctor in Montignac because she was ill. He said it was because of weakness in the stomach lining and said she must not eat acidy foods.

On the Saturday I took Mum to Bordeaux and put her on a plane (covered by insurance). She would have been happy to stay, but my sister Audrey was coming from America and she wanted to get back for that and I also felt I had enough to worry about. Still, I missed the company. It was fine during the day but lonely at night and I didn't sleep well, because I usually listened to the World Cup on the radio and the tension and excitement kept me awake. I did quite a lot of work and phoned the office and so on. Mel came over and we made further plans. The representative of the Total company came to talk about installing the central heating gas tank (buried in the garden by the cistern under the lime tree). Mel is a very good arranger. He knows his limitations and gets experts to do the difficult things. So the central heating lady was followed by M. Lascoumes, who will install the heating (we discussed the radiators etc.) and another man who examined the roof and woodwork in the grenier over the kitchen. He said there was no need to re-do the roof as the battens and tiles were generally in good condition. Mel has plans for using new material to insulate the room, which looked fine to me. Various quotes were submitted and accepted. Most of the work will begin in September – October.

The operation was on the Wednesday, a week after Heather was admitted. I went in the afternoon and she was still sore and drugged. Much the same next day, but by Friday she was feeling better, helped by bunches of flowers and cards (one bunch came from the office). The hospital staff were rather puzzled and wanted to know if it was a birthday – they don't go in for flowers at hospitals, it seems.

I worked away at some office work and sent that off on a diskette. Natasha[6] sent me some stuff on another diskette. I swam, did some gardening and went to the hospital. England made shaky progress in the Cup and I listened to them lose to Romania and then later redeem themselves with a splendid win over Colombia. The match against Argentina was the best match of the tournament so far, according to the pundits (and Roger Brière[7], whom I saw in town the next morning). Poor Beckham, villain of the hour.

Heather came out of hospital on Friday, 3 July. I drove her back and on the way stopped off in Rouffignac, where Dr Bardet gave us the name of a nurse who was to come and see Heather to change the dressings etc. I phoned her, but she said that it would be better to get someone more local, because she didn't want to poach on someone else's territory. So I phoned a Madame Sauliere, from Bars, who is the district nurse for the area. She came on Saturday afternoon. She was surprised that we didn't have any medical supplies with us, but the hospital didn't say we needed them. Mme S. went into Thenon and got what was necessary. In the meantime, a fair was being assembled in Thenon, with dodgem cars and rides crammed into every corner that was available. It opened on Sunday with a parade and included a firework display that night. I heard it – lots of bangs and thuds – but Heather was too tired to go. However, we shall remember it another year.

On Saturday, 4 July, a digger arrived. Mel had hired it to dig the hole for the gas tank. The earth from there was then dumped over by the ditch, the aim being to fill that in completely. He laid some pipes to take the water from the septic tank, putting a special access box in so that we could clear the pipes if they ever get blocked. Using the digger he then filled in the ditch. It had never occurred to Heather and me that this was an option – the ditch had always remained somehow sacrosanct, something you had to work round.

Mel had also cleared out the grenier and the little room next to it (good floors, some holes made by RB to put in lights etc). On Tuesday morning I made a bonfire of this and other rubbish. It all went up in the space of just over an hour and the whole site was now clear and we could see how it would look in the future – very nice indeed. I watered the plants on the bank. It is getting hot now and things are beginning to dry up. The pool gets hotter and hotter. Up to 28 degrees, by using the summer cover at nights.

* * *

1999

Somehow this whole year seems to have disappeared. I probably didn't have the computer fixed up when we were in France. One highlight of the year was that the car broke down on the way home. The exhaust pipe came off. I rang the AA in Calais and a truck was there (a motorway service station) within a few minutes. They loaded the car on board and took us to some place about ten miles away, but they didn't have a spare part. So we had to stay in a motel for a few days while they fixed it.

These are some notes made by my wife Heather for that year.

Easter 1999

We came on Wednesday, 31 March and Easter was early again. Once more glorious weather so we were able to burn the old apple tree at last (it had been blown down in a storm) and the walnut tree, which failed to survive the winter. We saw a hoopoe, but not in the garden, and we have heard a cuckoo. The swallows have arrived in Thenon and seem happy to swoop with abandon about the town. In our wood we have found morels, but have not dared to cook them, and violets. We found a fritillary – purpleish and another lemony white one – the first we have ever seen in the garden, and I was so pleased.

Under the horse chestnut tree are two wild orchids, so we are doing our bit for wildlife. What I have always assumed to be a larch that we saved by the ditch I now believe to be an elm and I have had the radical idea of chopping down the tree by the pool which causes so much trouble. No one else has commented as yet. Very little sound of night creatures this year but then Mel has been in doing the heating and the last room above the kitchen – our study and work room, with possible sleeping arrangements. It is a lovely room: the best in the house, I think.

Wednesday, 7 April 1999

This afternoon we saw a hoopoe displaying his reflection in the glass of the kitchen door. Spectacular! About five-ish.

Monday, 28 June 1999

The last Sunday of these holidays. Storms today water the plants wonderfully but put our electricity out for an hour or so. Who cares? We saw two deer in a field coming back from Perigueux last night, between Fossemagne and here and a red squirrel earlier in the day. M. Dartinset brought us some lettuce today, so we abandoned the idea of going out for Sunday lunch in favour of a last feast of all our left-overs, plus the lettuce. It was wonderful. Sylvie – the Dartinsets' grand-daughter - came and sported in the pool yesterday. What energy. Roger and I were exhausted just watching her.

September 1999

Our last week. We Eurostarred to Paris and stayed there, doing the Musée d'Orsay, and then trained to Brive and hired a car. Not brilliant weather, but very warm at times. A crack has opened by the door to the kitchen, which is worrying. We will keep an eye on it and get an expert in if it moves further. M. Dartinset seems to think it is to be expected in such old buildings and there is nothing to worry about.

I saw a praying mantis on the drive. It seems very pious, I must say (as the author of *The God of Small Things* would say), but when I tried the pool (22 degrees) it was too cold to stay in. We've bought white daffodils and tulips for the white alley behind the pool and everything is growing well. But only two out of six peonies are still growing so I have my doubts about them.

All over there are men in green with guns, so I expect the local wildlife has been decimated. Our figs are ripe but very wet and don't taste too good, unfortunately – but I persevere. We were woken frequently last night by what I though was the central heating, but Roger says it was the swift deaths of several of the local beasts – so much for the quiet of the countryside, he says.

I weeded around the house and the drive today and it is beginning to look good. We are perfecting our plans for the garden and saw some good trees to be planted at this time next year in Jardiland.

Monday, 27 September 1999

More of the garden done – the drive to the bend and the start of the tidying-up around vulnerable plants. Door and lock hinges oiled and working smoothly, various brambles clipped. We planted the daffodils, tulips and narcissi in that order (daffs nearest the house).

* * *

Saturday, 17 June 2000

It is a glorious morning; sunny, with a breeze blowing from the northeast. The temperature should reach 33 degrees today, according to the Sud - Ouest,[8] and the pool is already 27 degrees (up from 21 on Saturday). This is our first holiday since I retired, and we are both enjoying it – perhaps it is the feeling that we can come again whenever we like. Yesterday Nita, Judith and Maurice[9] came to dinner. They are down here because Nita is selling her house and she asked me to go and speak to M. Bonnie, the notaire, about the legal aspects. It all seems fairly straightforward.

We have been doing various things – going to supermarkets, M. Bricolage[10] and so on, our usual holiday pleasures. Tomorrow we go on our one-week painting holiday at the Chateau de Brâ, near Altillac in Correze. No real problems here. Mel has been living here, so his things are all over the place – his own house is being renovated, so he has had to get out. While we are here he is living at the Smiths. He is putting in a terrace for us near the entrance. Paving steps, in wide gradual steps. It looks very good and will transform the entrance, which is the least attractive part of the property. We think we will put some bulbs and perhaps shrubs on the other side of the entrance and during the summer we will plant busy lizzies or geraniums or other annuals in pots on the new terrace. The old cistern cover has been dragged to the edge of the drive and we can fill that with plants as well. It will make the downstairs room one of the most attractive, because the view outside will be so pretty, especially as you can open the French windows and walk outside from there.

The garden had a bit of a pasting during the storm of December 1999. The cherry tree fell down and crushed the compost heap and several other trees came down as well, leaving the wood looking rather empty. There are several stumps lying on the lawn near M. Barbini's[11] field, waiting to be burnt, and there are large holes in the lawn where stumps have been removed. It will recover with time. I scattered grass seed on the bare patches, just in time for the rain to end and the sun to come out. No rain this week, so I expect the grass seed will be feeling the strain by now.

I have been looking at motor mowers. Husqvarna have a new shop in what used to be the furniture shop on the N89, by the turning to Ajat. The trouble is they are so noisy. So I have decided to get a Honda from Motoplaisance in Perigueux. The price is about 16,000 francs.

I have put up my hammock in the garden, between two trees. It is very comfortable and it is difficult to stay awake once you are in it.

I am typing this waiting for two phone calls – one is from M. Cestari, the pool man. The cleaner doesn't work properly. There is very little pressure and so the suction is not strong enough to suck up the dirt. I am also waiting a call from Natasha, who is on her way to Spain with the family and is staying at the Club Med village near Pompadour, about an hour or so away from here. She said she would phone this morning, but it is now 11am and we haven't heard. We might go over this afternoon anyway.

Sunday, 18 June 2000

We did go over to Pompadour. Natasha phoned and we went there after trying and failing to find a craft fair at Mayac (we think it might have been a different Mayac) and then going to Terrasson to see about the pool. M. Marchive was there, chatting to some new clients; he said he would arrange for someone to come. He duly arrived quite early on Sunday morning and we had a look at the motor. There was a lot of water in the unit, and he drained this by drilling two holes in the bottom. He will come during the week – I left him a key to the cave.

We were quite impressed with Pompadour. The Club Med set-up was very slick and efficient and had something for everyone, although it was clearly aimed at families; swimming pool, mini golf course, horse riding and tennis lessons. It was very French and so the food was good. We waited for Natasha and Nacho to arrive in the bar but of course were not allowed to buy any drinks because we did not have vouchers (no cash is allowed – a bit of an affectation, but probably people like it). We ate there and had a very good buffet-style meal, with four courses and as much as you could eat. But at about 9.15pm everyone started to leave and by 9.30pm the restaurant was virtually empty. Quite strict discipline, underneath the 1950s-1960s hippy exterior. As we left there was a Redcoat-style floorshow; the staff all dressed up in their 1960s gear and singing 'Flower Power' songs.

We took Nita, Maurice and Judith to the Ferme de Layotte on Thursday. We had booked, but we were the only ones there. The waiter, we gathered, was also the cook and owner. Very charming, rather natty with his Napoleon III beard and moustache. He offered us an aperitif made of cherry leaves and our starter was a pâté of pork or smoked pork (the latter was the better), followed by two meats, including kidneys. Local home-made cheeses and a lovely cake of nuts, with various sauces made from fruits. All beautifully presented. The waiter's wife and child came down the stairs later. I wondered how they all got on, so isolated and surrounded by nature. It would take very special people to like that environment for long, but they seemed very well and thriving on it. The meal was 145 francs a head, including wine and other drinks.

Off painting this afternoon. Both are looking forward to it.

We are thinking about the garden, etc. The new terrace by the downstairs room will transform the approach. H. wants a little box-type hedge between the area where the gas tank is and the driveway itself. That seems a good idea to me. We also think Russian vines or something similar could go over the house on the prairie[12] and perhaps some more laurels by the front of the pool on the other side of the gate. The only part of the pool that is not screened is where the gate is. The far end, where the japonicas are, and the sides, near yucca corner and the south side, could also do with some more plants. Possibly some honeysuckle, because it grows quickly and likes it here and gives off such a wonderful fragrance. The old laurels and the shrubs on the north side are all well established now and look lovely – they not only give privacy but make the pool look beautiful.

Sunday, 25 June 2000

Rather cold, overcast. A change from the first week here. We spent the last week at Chateau de Brâ, near Beaulieu in Correze, where we were on our painting holiday. It was a triumph! The castle, owned by Edward and Alex Roch (the latter being our teacher) is a beautifully restored building in its own park, complete with huge swimming pool. We had an apartment in a converted stable block across the courtyard from the main building. We were not sure what to expect and Heather was a little doubtful about going at all, because we had no idea who else was going or what the standard would be. In the event we needn't have worried. The two others on the course were Pam from Cookham and Caroline from Edinburgh, both very nice in different ways.

On the first day we stayed at the chateau and went off to sketch different bits. I did a wall with a statue and didn't like the result at all. Alex came over – she usually goes to each person once in the morning and once in the afternoon – and suggested that I needed to pick the focal point and then work out from there rather than try to do everything at the start. I should use a notebook to sketch in the highlights and tones and generally work out the composition etc. I found this very useful. I did a drawing of a banana tree by the pool and then another drawing of a spring, which I liked a lot. Heather, meanwhile, was doing another view and she also found Alex's advice very good. Like revelations, really!

The next day we set off for some fields near Gragnac, where we sketched landscapes. Heather had discovered watercolour crayons and liked them a lot. The results were very strong and rather un-watercolour-like. I tried doing some drawings and pastels of the distant hills, but was not very happy with the results. Then I did a pencil drawing of the lane where I was sitting. I tried to keep it quite simple, just using line, and the result was very pleasing. I felt I was beginning to make progress. We went into Gragnac after a very pleasant picnic lunch and did more pictures of buildings. Heather did some excellent line drawings, very strong and clear, and we returned to Brâ quite elated at our progress. The food at the castle was wonderful – very simple but always spot-on – and we really enjoyed the pool, which was 28 degrees all the time we were there. It had an automatic cleaner fitted, which intrigued us all. It crawled all over the pool cleaning away while the surface dirt was simply swept over the side into a tank where it was filtered and recycled.

We went to Bretenoux the next day, where I did a pastel of water going over a weir and Heather did a similar view from the other side, with buildings in the background, followed by a watercolour of water going over rocks. She was very pleased, because the picture really came out well. Alex again proved her talent as a teacher, because Heather was worried that the top part of her picture was too dark. Alex suggested lightening the bottom by blotting out some of the painting there. It worked a treat. We had a picnic there and carried on in the afternoon. It was our best day so far and we both felt we had discovered a hobby that would give great pleasure for years to come. Swimming in the evening then out to dinner at Gragnac Port (280 francs for two of us).

We stayed around the house the next day (Thursday) because some new people had arrived. Mike is the artist, while his wife and her cousin were there for walks and sightseeing. Alex always likes to start people close to the house because there is plenty to paint there and it helps them to find their feet a bit. I did the gate leading into the chateau in the morning and then in the afternoon did the steps near the pool. Caroline, our jolly Scottish friend, did them in the morning – great dashes of colour, very different to her normal work. I think she was feeling a bit liberated, like us. Pam, meanwhile, was proving herself to be the most accomplished painter, with some exquisitely painted landscapes, very delicate and well observed. But even she then did some very vigorous paintings, including one of the drive to the house that surprised us all. I tried to do a picture of an old horse carriage but found it difficult to do the wheel, which I was looking at from an angle so that it was more of an ellipse than a circle. Measure the spokes, said Alex, and after that it became easier. It's surprising how much the angle does distort things. Heather, meanwhile, was having great fun doing pictures of trees, mainly using the crayons.

On Friday we went to Beaulieu riverside, which was full of subjects to paint. Heather and Caroline painted the old church by the river, while I did a house not far away. Then we went back to Brâ for lunch and in the afternoon I finished off the steps. I think I liked it best of my efforts, because there was a lot of colour in it, not just the usual detailed drawing.

We took Caroline back to Brive the next day to catch the train and we all talked about going to Brâ again next year. It was such a lovely place, comfortable, warm welcome, perfect food and good companions. Alex was quite inspirational as a teacher. She could spot our errors very easily and then suggest an instant correction.

We got back to Le J. at about 10am and immediately set off to Perigueux to get some food. We saw Mel on our return, who said he had checked mowers and the one I wanted could be delivered on Tuesday. He has almost finished the terrace by the entrance – it looks really good – and has mended the upstairs loo. So we went off to Perigueux in the afternoon and ordered the mower, then went to Perigueux for a coffee, bought some paints and thought about going there in the evening for dinner but were too tired. We stopped at Jardiland on the way home and bought some compost and plants. We intend to fill the old cistern head, which is now on the edge of the driveway, with geraniums.

We ate at home and saw M. Barbini out in the field getting in the hay. He had cut it while we were away and was now bundling it into large round bales. They finished at about 8pm. I went and said hello. They were rather intrigued by all the work we have been doing.

It is now 6.10pm. A dull cloudy day, a bit brighter now and warmer than it was earlier. We went out this afternoon to get some compost and plants for the old cistern head. It looks a lot better now, but still needs a few more plants – Jardiland had run out of geraniums, thanks partly to our venture there the day before. Sylvie came over to show us her tame mouse, a pretty little thing that whizzes round its own treadmill.

On the way back from Jardiland we went via Les Eyzies and the Côte du Jôr. It seems as though a new extension is being added to the museum and there is now a little bus-train that goes up and down the main street, carrying solemn-faced tourists. The view from the Côte du Jôr has now been cleared away at one point and it is quite breathtaking. You can see the castle at St Leon and also the tower of the church at Sergeac. I didn't have my camera with me but we plan to go back and take some shots. I like the idea of doing a large pastel of it.

Monday, 18 September 2000

This time we came down on the train, stopping in Paris for two nights on the way. We stayed at a very nice hotel called the Residence Imperiale, which is very close to the Porte Maillot Metro station. We were a bit worried about whether we would get away at all because the blockade of petrol stations only ended a few days before and we thought we might be stranded. In the event I was able to fill Heather's car up on Thursday, after queuing for an hour at Whitehill Service Station. That meant Jenny[13] had one car with a full tank to see her through the week. On the way to Ashford I filled up at the petrol station near Leeds. We were very early – about 6.30am – and there weren't many cars around. The Eurostar trip was uneventful. We got a taxi from the Gare du Nord and in the afternoon went on a coach trip to Versailles. The gardens still show the damage from the storm of last December. Many trees were destroyed and are now being replaced but there is obviously a lot of work still to be done. There were lots of people there, including many Japanese, and we waited with them for the musical water display to start. Not wildly exciting. The fountains duly started at 3pm, accompanied by Mozart,

Handel, etc. It made a very nice atmosphere and we walked around the various water features, wondering what Charlie Dimmock would make of it all. Then back to the palace for the grand tour. We followed crowds of people who were following tour leaders waving umbrellas, parasols or flags, from room to room. Every so often a group would stop and gather round the leader who would explain the rituals of the royal breakfast etc. Each room led directly into the next – no corridors, therefore no privacy. Apparently anyone could wander around Versailles as long as he was wearing a sword and a hat, which could be hired outside.

Although I have been before, this was the first time I found myself becoming angry at the sheer extravagance of Versailles. How much did it cost the state to build and maintain? How far was that cost to blame for the revolution a hundred years later?

We got back to the hotel about 7pm, which gave us just enough time for a bit of a rest and then out to dinner. The hotel in the Avenue de Malakoff was very well placed for eating and we went to a restaurant called the Congrès Maillot, which specialised in fish and shellfish. Despite this, I had lamb and Heather had magret de canard. Both delicious, although my lamb was a little too pink for my liking. We both had G and Ts to start with (50 francs each) and the total bill came to 514 francs. The lamb was 129 Fr, the duck 98, a bottle of the house red Bordeaux was 94 and we both had desserts (Heather nougat ice and me profiteroles). Very good value.

The next day (Monday) we went off to the Pompidou Centre, which wasn't open (not until 11am) so we walked down to Notre Dame and joined the other tourists in a slow shuffle around the darkened aisles. Very big and oppressive. It must have been intimidating in the Middle Ages, when people were more religious than they are now. The Japanese all seem to insist on taking pictures of each other in front of something interesting. Fortunately, they are not very big, otherwise you wouldn't be able to see what they were standing in front of. By the time we had finished and had a coffee it was time for Pompidou, so off we went. We decided not to go to the Picasso sculpture exhibition but went to the general exhibition, which was wonderful. It began more or less where the Musée d'Orsay leaves off, in other words at about 1900, when the Post-Impressionists, Fauvists, Cubists and Surrealists were taking over. We went up to the 5th floor on the still rather exciting escalators on the outside of the building. The advantage of having the piping and escalators on the outside is that the inside is virtually free for the exhibits themselves, and what exhibits they are. The museum has one big advantage in being in Paris, which was the centre of world art until about 1950. You cannot really study that period without going to the Pompidou. We were both bowled over by it all, and at the same time exhausted, so we didn't really see much on the 4th floor (art after 1950, basically). We'll do that another time.

We found a little café where we both had salads (very filling) and then we got the Metro to La Defense (like Maillot it is on line 1), which is a bit like Canary Wharf and gives a spectacular view of the Arc de Triomphe. Then back to the hotel for a lie down, before going out to eat at a restaurant just up the road from the hotel (I think it was called del Papa; anyway it was Italian). Very good and not too expensive. Then back to the hotel, watched a bit of the Olympics on the telly and then to sleep.

Tuesday, 19 September 2000

Off to Gare d'Austerlitz for the 10.15 train to Brive. We had used up the last of our ten tickets (for 58 francs) so had to buy two singles. The train was quite full but the journey was pleasant, although by the time we got to Brive the weather had changed and it was raining. Apparently it has been a very dry summer, and warm as well. We picked up our hire car (a small Daewoo, rather slow and uninspiring, from Hertz), did some shopping at Intermarché in Terrasson and got to the house at about 4pm. We tried to find Mel's number but while we were doing so he rang us and arranged to come over in the morning. We unpacked, toured the garden (looking good – Mel had been and mowed the lawn), had some microwaved frozen cannelloni (very good it was too) and read for a while before bed. Both tired out. But both agreed that the two days in Paris were perfect.

Wednesday, 20 September 2000

Mel came as arranged and we discussed various things, including the crack. He will get two builders to have a look at it. There is also a problem with the mower, which has two punctures. The front right wheel is currently being repaired and when that is done the back wheel will have to be fixed. Why they should have punctures is a mystery. Probably something to do with the seal rather than a straight puncture. Anyway, it means I won't be able to play with it this time.

There is also a small leak in the liner of the pool. As a result the water level goes down gradually. We have to get Desjoyaux to come and do the *hivernage*, so I shall get them to mend it at the same time.

I prepared a list of jobs for Mel. I tried to print this list out, but the printer has gone haywire and keeps spewing out fonts and general gobbledegook as if it is on a prolonged self-test. It wastes paper and ink and time. I managed to sort out the problem in the end. The default printer was set as the Epson 8000 that I now have at home. Once I selected the HP Deskjet 520 all was well. Now all I've got to do is get rid of all that wasted paper.

In the afternoon we went in to Thenon and ordered a new fridge from the little shop where we bought the washing machine. The one we want is not in stock so will be delivered to us tomorrow at 8.15am.

Thursday, 21 September 2000

The new fridge has been delivered. It turned out to be a long job, because it was about 0.5 cm too tall to get under the cupboard where we wanted it. Then the electrician said that we should make our system safer and bring it up to modern standards. I asked him to do it, which he duly did. We have put the new fridge on the other side of the kitchen and have moved the table back to its old position by the garden windows. The electrician, whose wife runs the shop, told us a little more about the tempest. It was very frightening and lasted from 8pm to 1am in the morning. He was still shaking for weeks afterwards, he said. Trees, electricity and telephone lines were down everywhere. M. Dartinset said that a relative of his from Bars was at their house that night. She decided that she could not get home in her car, so she left it at the Dartinsets. She asked Jean-Paul for a lift, but he said that if she couldn't make it in her car, how could he make it in his? So she went by foot and had a traumatic journey, with trees crashing all round her in the darkness.

One thing that has come out of it is that the telephone line, that used to hang as low as the kitchen window, has now been raised. I have to go into Thenon tomorrow afternoon to pay the bills.

Heather

I have just come in from the garden where I saw what I think, and hope, was a grass snake, sunning itself in the long grass at the very edge of our wood. It stayed quite still, and so did I, and then gradually eased itself back to the safety of our wood. I shall certainly wear wellingtons if ever go there again! It must have been two feet long and was a darkish sludgy green with darker blotches along its back. The book says they sometimes have yellow and/or orange colours near their neck but I was too surprised to take that much notice and so cannot confirm or deny. The grapes near where it was are small and black and very sweet to eat, which was what I was doing there in the first place.

Later the same day: I was simply taking a walk around the estate this evening, at eight-ish, when I saw a deer in the prairie behind our wood. Naturally, it heard me and the barking dog from the farm, and rushed off towards the wood by the electricity pylons. I could see that it was female, and that it didn't really seem to be too worried as it stopped from time to time to gaze back at me. When it moved it made small leaps in the air, and it went along the edge of M. Barbini's field where the strawberries were. How exciting.

Friday, 22 September 2000

Most of the plants are okay, but the honeysuckle by the pool has gone brown and is clearly in a bad way. Heather thinks it might be the salt water from the pool. However, the ceanothus by the corner of the house is also struggling. Maybe it is the dry weather that is to blame. The new paved area outside the downstairs room looks excellent – very nicely done, neat and clean. It has transformed that room, which is now very pleasant indeed and is also quite warm, now that the central heating is on. The sun is shining this morning (10.50am) but there is a slight wind and it is chilly first thing and in the shade. The good weather is supposed to continue until at least Sunday.

We waited in most of the day for Mel, who didn't arrive. So in the afternoon we went to Terrasson to arrange for the hivernage and also to pay for the fridge. The shop in Thenon is owned by M. and Mme Jean-Marc Lespinasse and one reason why we bought it from them is that they are such nice people – we got the washing machine there as well. It is an Arthur Martin model and cost 3,000 francs. To fix the electricity cost another 901 francs. One curiosity was that when they turned the electricity back on the lights in the new study upstairs were not properly on – just a very dim light. It turned out that they had been connected to the general circuit rather than the lights. M. Lespinasse and his colleague fixed it for us.

At Desjoyaux we paid the bill and then we bought a repair kit for the small leak in the liner. It cost about 46 francs and we fixed it when we got home. Simply cut a small circle out of the PVC supplied (not a square – I suppose circles fix better) and then apply a dab of glue in the centre. Then press it over the leak and hold it down for a minute. A bit like mending a bicycle puncture. It seemed to work.

The water temperature is about 20 degrees. But it felt quite warm. Heather says she might go for a swim tomorrow. I shall think about it. (It got up to 22 degrees by the time the cover went on tonight.)

Dinner at the Mule Blanche. Total bill was 342 francs, two meals at 120 francs and a bottle of St Exupery Pecharmant at 102 francs. We ate out on the terrace and enjoyed it very much. There was a cheaper menu at 100 and another at 153 but we felt we would not be able to eat it all. We still cannot figure out how they can produce such good food so cheaply. The hotel is obviously doing well because they have just finished the new terrace by the entrance (opened in June). Our menu started with a soup, followed by foie gras (very rich) and then confit de canard, some cabecou (we could have had other cheeses) and finally a dessert of chocolate cake with crème anglaise. Perfect. I had indigestion all night, despite lots of Rennies.

Saturday, 23 September 2000

A leisurely day. Very sunny and warm. White lacy clouds began to gather in the afternoon. Does that mean rain tomorrow, as the weather forecast suggests? I rang Mel, who says he will come tomorrow between 10 and 11am, so we went off the Perigueux in the afternoon to visit Jardiland and get a few things from Leclerc (a lightbulb, some food, a film). We decided not to swim after all. We sat by the pool instead and read books and dozed, without feeling at all guilty. Then we had a little bonfire.

Sylvie came over this evening. It is her birthday today (fourteen) and she had some friends round to celebrate. She is growing up fast and is very pretty.

I read *The Remorseful Day,* the last *Morse,* and started the *Dictionary of the Khazars,* a very odd book but quite engrossing.

Sunday, 24 September 2000

A bit cloudy this morning, but the forecast on the BBC website for Bordeaux is for sunshine between now and Thursday, so we remain optimistic.

On Thursday, the Dartinsets had their *vendange.* Heather saw M. D. when she went to post a letter and he showed her the huge vat with the wine in. Not a very good year, he told her. The quantity is not so great as normal. That is probably because it has been such a dry year that the grapes have not had a chance to swell. I wonder what that means for the harvest in general – low in quantity but high in quality? Or low in both?

Mel came round and we talked about things to do. He says he has got someone coming round to look at the crack. I told him I needed two estimates, so he will get someone else as well. He is moving to a new place near St Orse.

We had Sunday lunch at the Soleil d'Or. Very good meal (the menu was called the Chateau de Losse, for 153 francs). Basically the same as the next one up, but you had to choose between the fish and the meat. It was plenty for us. Heather had the fish which was salmon and was very good, she says, while I had carré d'agneau. Rather pink, but that's the way they like it down here. We only drank half the bottle of wine, so we had it corked up again and brought it home for tonight.

We saw Roger Brière on the way home. He was limping very badly so his operation has not solved all his problems. Then we saw Mel, who had left a plant catalogue at the house for us. RB says that the only thing to do when you get subsidence is to rebuild the affected part – if you underpin, then you can still get problems of movement, because the clay expands and contracts, depending on the moisture level.

Monday, 25 September 2000

Heather's cold has got worse if anything. We cancelled our trip to Perigueux and went back to Thenon where I bought various potions. Then we went back to the house and she sat by the pool. Fortunately, it is a lovely autumn day, very warm, clear blue sky. The lady in the chemist told me it was very bad weather in England. "So you should stay here," she said, smiling. "I am afraid we have things to do," I replied. The train leaves Brive at 9.57pm, so we have plenty of time to get there.

The potions seem to have worked. Heather's head cleared and after lunch (a salad by the pool) we went off to Perigueux to buy a present for Jenny and something for Sylvie. It was quite sleepy in town. Lots of shops were shut and the weather, while lovely, had a very definite autumn feel about it. It is a different season here. At home summer just slides into autumn and autumn into winter without you knowing it.

* * *

Monday, 9 April 2001

We arrived yesterday for our Easter break. Had an excellent trip down, caught the 7.45am ferry and were here by 5.30pm, not tired at all. The house was in good condition. The crack in the kitchen wall seemed no worse than last year, which was just as well because Mel hasn't done anything and seems to have vanished. His phone is disconnected and Roger Brière hasn't seen him since before Christmas.

Last night we went to the Soleil d'Or and had the Chateau de Losse menu (now 160 francs). Very nicely cooked and good value. We started with asparagus and I had magret de canard for the main course, followed by cabecou and a rich chocolate dessert.

We saw Roger in Thenon and although he was limping he seems to be much better and much more cheerful. He was complaining about too much work and people who don't pay on time. The Dartinsets all seem to be well. Sylvie came this afternoon and Heather gave her her Easter egg – a pretty red bag which Sylvie seemed to like very much.

We spent the morning cleaning the house etc. but my part was a bit disappointing. I managed to get the mower working (I pulled out the choke and it started!) but it turned out to have a flat front tyre. Mel had told me about it and said he would fix it, but he didn't. We took it to Perigueux this afternoon but Motoplaisance was closed. We went to the France Telecom office because our upstairs line has been disconnected (by Mel) but that was closed as well. So we shall have to go again tomorrow morning.

So it was all a bit frustrating. However, we have two weeks, so no panic as yet.

Tuesday, 10 April 2001

Another overcast morning, quite cold as well. Yesterday we went off to Perigueux and I took the tyre back to Motoplaisance, who said it will be ready about 6pm today. It was. But the wheel was damaged and they had to put an inner tube in. I think Mel must have gone too fast and hit something, because the wheel was badly dented and that is how the air came out. We had another try for France Telecom and found they have moved their office to the Rue Taillefer, which is on the edge of the old city centre, not far from the cathedral. The lady there said I could phone up (10 14) which is a free phone number, but I explained that, in addition to the phone extension the line itself was so bad we couldn't hear properly, so we used her phone and got through to the service people who promised that someone will come between 10 and 12 next Wednesday. So both our priority items are under control.

We still have the crack in the wall, however. It looks much the same as it did last year and I think the wet weather has helped to stabilise it. However, it still needs to be fixed. But who will do it? There must be people around who can do this. I shall go to the Syndicat d'Initiatif and see if they have a list. We need someone to look after the garden as well as do jobs about the house.

The honeysuckle and ceanothus are both dead, so we went to Perigueux yesterday and bought some more plants. The house over the road is crumbling still further. Any minute now the roof will give way completely.

I brought my French with me and have done a bit of that. In my first TMA I got 82% for the written and 76% for the oral. Too many careless mistakes though.

On our various trips to Perigueux we have seen the first signs of the new autoroute, which will run from Clermont-Ferrand to Bordeaux. Some of the woods around Eyliac have been cleared and work is now proceeding on what appears to be a major interchange. According to the *Sud-Ouest* today some of the people near Terrasson are not very happy because the new road will not run through a long tunnel as they had hoped but only in a short one, so much of it will be exposed. Their objections are much the same as they are everywhere else – NIMBY. But they probably have a case, because apparently the new maps are different to the ones they saw originally. The job will probably take several years to complete and by the time it is finished we won't be able to remember what it looked like in the first place.

Sunday, 15 April 2001

A fine, sunny day, but chilly. Yesterday was also fine, but the cold wind from the north kept the temperature down. I bought a new *debroussailleuse* (garden strimmer) from Husqvarna, the other one having mysteriously disappeared. It cost about £250. We also need a new wheelbarrow, as the old one has gone and we have been left with a barrow with no wheel. We had an aperitif with the Smiths last evening and plan to go out with them for dinner on Tuesday. They say that Isabelle is no longer at the restaurant. She has gone away, which is what her mother told me last year. There must have been some sort of row, or maybe Isabelle just felt she should break free from the family and get a life of her own. Today Heather is in some pain because she seems to have pulled a groin muscle. She got up at just after 7am because lying down was painful. I got up too. To show solidarity. Which is why I am sitting here typing this at 8.30am.

Yesterday was spent gardening. Jenny and Heather worked very hard and I got the mower out and drove around. The garden looks so much bigger when the grass is mown and the mower is very good in the wood, since it chops down the weeds and brambles.

Tuesday, 17 April 2001

We went to the market today. Not as big as it used to be. Maybe that is just the season, but I think that it is part of the general decline of rural France. There are lots of empty shops in Thenon and a good summer season won't help much in a town that doesn't attract many tourists. The weather is not too bad. Today is sunny, but there is a cold wind at times and there was a frost this morning. We bought a few plants and have planted them out. There is a ceanothus on the bank (by Gertrude Jekyll, which is looking very unhappy) and we put a spiraea there as well. We put a broom at the end of the pool and a wisteria at the house end by the gate.

The new debroussailleuse works well, although I couldn't get it to start until Douglas showed up. He told me what to do and it started. I then went with him to look at his new machine, which also wouldn't start, probably because the mixture of oil and petrol was too rich. I told him to pull the choke out, after which it worked. So we both felt smug. It is now 12.30pm. Heather and Jenny are reading and I might go and do the same.

Monday, 11 June 2001

Back for our summer holiday. We spent the first week of the month at the Chateau de Brâ, where we went last year. Mima[14] came with us and we all had a very nice time. They are so friendly and hospitable. A very nice group of people, including David Green, a retired accountant from Devon, Diana Hollis, who works for Phillips, and a French lady called Paulette who spends the year, it seems, going on painting holidays. We were quite lucky with the weather, which was dry at least, although not always baking hot. Still, it has been worse in England. We took Mima back to Brive today and put her on the 9.37am train to Paris. We did a bit of shopping on the way back and have been doing a bit of spring cleaning since then. The pool was not very clean, so we have been vacuuming that and it is a bit better now. The mower needs a bit of attention, I think. Maybe the valve needs cleaning or the oil changing. I'll have a look at it. The temperature in the sun was 29 degrees a few minutes ago. Apparently it hit 34 degrees two weeks ago, which must have been unbearable.

Tuesday, 12 June 2001

Charles and Kelly[15] arrived yesterday and we took them to the Commanderie at Condat for a very nice meal. Today we sat around a lot and then went to Lascaux for the English tour, which was very interesting. The pool is getting cleaner. The trouble is that stuff comes down from the tree and collects on the bottom. It is easy enough to vacuum, but it clogs the filter bag so you have to keep changing it. Another very hot day, blue skies etc. It is not so good in England. Oh dear.

Today M. Martinez came to fix the leaking pipe by the washing machine (recommended by M. Dartinset). He was only here about fifteen minutes and fixed it. It cost 120 francs – v. cheap.

Wednesday, 13 June 2001

The temperature reached 35 degrees in the sun at lunchtime and the pool temperature rose to 26 by the same time. It really is very hot, with not much wind. We are all exhausted; don't know why, except for the heat. I went to the Mairie this morning to collect some new dustbin bags – for recycling waste. There is a special wheely bin for this. Rather like the blue bag system recently introduced at home. Tonight we think we shall go out, perhaps to a relatively cheap and unpretentious restaurant in Montignac. We are all feeling a little bloated. Last night we ate here, a roast veal joint that was very good. Some smoked salmon to start with, potatoes and carrots with the meat, then cheese and strawberries.

Friday, 15 June 2001

Charles and Kelly left this morning at about 9am. We went to the Soleil d'Or last night and had a lovely meal for 130 francs, sitting on a new outdoor terrace by the pool. I had raging indigestion all night and still feel bloated. The others are all complaining as well. It will be quite good to get back to normal food.

Today it is overcast and there was rain during the night. A hint of thunder in the air (as forecast). We plan to tidy up, etc.

An annoying problem with the mower. The battery has discharged. Motoplaisance sold me a charger but I could not get the cover off the battery compartment. There are two screws which are a bit like Allen key locks and need special keys, which Motoplaisance don't sell and I could not get them anywhere else either. I have written a snotty letter to Honda in France and an email to Honda in the UK. It means we shall have to leave the mower with a flat battery until we come down again later in the year.

The farmers are all rushing to get the hay in. M. Barbini has not started on his field yet, but I can hear a tractor outside the Dartinsets' farm, so I imagine he will be doing so fairly soon.

Monday, 22 October 2001

Four months have passed since my last diary entry, partly because I forgot to take the disc home with me. Since then a lot has happened. We came down in the spring of this year and in June, but neither of us was very well. Jenny came in the spring and did most of the driving. In the summer I drove, but I didn't feel very bright and in July I went to the doctor to say I was worried about my balance. He gave me some pills, which didn't work, and in August I went to see a specialist at Fawkham Manor (with Dr Zala's blessing) and he (Dr Zoukos) sent me off for blood tests and a scan. They cost about £750 each (for scans and blood test). This showed that I had a tumour on the brain. He arranged for me to see a surgeon in Harley St called M. Bullock and on 31 August I was in King's College Hospital, Denmark Hill, being operated on. Whilst there, I managed to collect a chest infection, which proved for a week or so to be worse than the tumour.

Now I am safely out and feeling better, but my balance is still bad and I find the stairs a bit of a challenge. Heather has developed a very nice cold and I am glad I brought the Night Nurse with me. Jenny is here and did all the driving.

We went to E. Leclerc at Perigueux today for some shopping and I am trying to phone M. Subresi, who has been recommended by M. Dartinset as a good mason. He can do the crack in the wall, I hope. He was not there last time I phoned (not back from lunch yet). Will try again soon.

Apart from that all seems well. Jan[16] has been because the grass down by M. Barbini's field has been cut and looks good. He hasn't cut the lawn but it doesn't need it. M. Barbini's field has been mown, by the way.

Jan drove us to Perigueux today. We bought a vacuum cleaner at Leclerc. H. says it is wonderful. That is part of the problem with bringing things from England – if they are not good enough for there, why should they be good enough for here?

Tuesday, 23 October 2001

10.35am French time. I have just got up. It is pouring with rain and H. and J. have gone to the market. They will get bread while they are there and we will have breakfast when they get back. M. Subresi from Renomat was supposed to come yesterday evening about the crack in the kitchen wall but he did not arrive. Mel got in touch with him some time ago and he gave an estimate for around £4,000, so I expect it will be a bit more now. I don't care. We have budgeted for it.

Jan did arrive and we talked about the garden. I gave him 600 francs for work he has done and he said he preferred it that way. He doesn't like being paid in advance, in case he doesn't do something.

He said he could cut down the two trees in the garden, the dying cherry and the one by the pool, which is lovely, but in the wrong position. Its leaves are all over the lawn and they clog up the pool and the patio around it. I am going to give Jan the keys to the shed and the mower so that he can use them when we are not here. He is a very nice man, very reliable and I would like him to take charge of things when we are not here.

I took the deeds to M. Labaisse but naturally now we are here, and despite the weather, we don't want to sell at all. We'll see how we feel next year. Either way, we are in profit. It really is nice here. The *fouines* (stone martens) got in, via the roof. They managed to crap on the top of the stairs leading to the downstairs room, but only from on high, and they seemed to leave their calling cards on the steps leading down to the kitchen. We must try to get some wire to block up the hole from the roof and also make sure we leave all the doors closed when we go home on Sunday.

Apart from the crack in the wall, everything is fine. I managed to open the mower cover (it takes the third smallest Imperial measurement, not a Continental one) but the extension lead would not extend to the house, so we shall have to push the mower out, one day when it is not raining. We might get another extension lead. Anyway, Jan seems to know about these things, so I can leave it for him if the worst comes to the worst. He has mowed the area below the bank by M. Barbini's field, but says it is too stony to do much with. Maybe we can buy some trees and plant them this time. Another trip to Jardiland…

We intended today to be a quiet one. I have fixed up the piano and the PC is fine. Might do a bit of drawing if I can. But we won't be outside very much. The CompuServe weather forecast for Brive says rain today and tomorrow and after that mixed, which is what it forecast (correctly) for Saturday, Sunday and Monday. So it looks as though tomorrow will be another quiet day as well.

We plan to go out for a meal tonight. We might go to Maria's. Alan[17] had a very good meal there in the summer, even though Isabelle has moved on. She went off to Sarlat with a man last year after a row with her parents. She is still there, but with a different man.

In the event, we stayed in and had a meal at home. Very nice too.

Just as we were going to bed, about 10pm, Viv[18] phoned to say Mum was in hospital. She apparently fell down stairs or had a stroke. Anyway, she was taken off to the very crowded accident and emergency ward on Monday, not remembering anyone or anything. By Tuesday night she was better, but still in hospital. Viv says no need to go home but we think we will go back on Saturday and not Sunday as planned. It is now lunchtime and the sun is shining. It took a long time to come through the morning mist. We think we will probably go back on Sunday after all. I have done a note for Jan but might change it. It depends on how I get on with the mower battery. I tried to repair the second bulb in the cave. But it broke. Another job for next time. It is a real mess in there. H. and J. are working in the garden. Every time I try to help I feel I am going to fall over, so I gave up. I rang Viv and she seems okay and I rang the hospital and Mum seems okay as well.

Maria's was shut this evening and apparently every evening. So we went to the Mule Blanche and had the Menu Perigourdin for 120 francs. Very nice. Confit de canard, which was very nice, and foie gras to start with.

M. Subresi came in the afternoon and he will submit another estimate – he had not been inside the house when Mel spoke to him. His original estimate was for 34,000 francs, so Mel had added well over 6,000 francs when he sent the estimate to us. He said that most of the problem was due to the downpipe from the roof which pours water straight into the ground. This keeps it very wet under the wall and makes movement inevitable. He wants to put a trench down the drive to the field below.

Thursday, 25 October 2001

Went to see RB on our way shopping this morning. He seems well, but his left hip is playing up. He is off to the Pyrenées with some friends next weekend. Jerome is in New York. Paule is on a course about the euro. I told him about my operation. A very dull, misty start to the day. But the forecast is for sun this afternoon, which seems quite possible.

The forecast was correct. We had lunch (a thick, leek soup made by Jenny) by the pool and watched the air force planes fly noisily overhead. I put the mower battery on charge, connecting it to the main in the house, and in the afternoon it started, much to my relief. I rushed off to amend my note to Jan. We are eating in tonight. The ladies feel the need for something rather less fattening.

Friday, 26 October 2001

A beautiful day. Clouds very high up, but it is sunny and the morning mist disappeared very quickly. We have been walking and sitting in the sun by the pool – very relaxing. It is a perfect autumn. We are waiting for the Smiths to arrive, perhaps this evening. I have got the mower working and will leave Jan instructions and a set of keys. It is a bonus having tomorrow here as well – we are returning early on Sunday.

Saturday, 27 October 2001

Our last day. It is very clear and a little chilly in the shade. The central heating has been a blessing. It was set on "night" so that it would come on if the temperature dropped to 5 degrees but of course it didn't. We turned it up to "day" and then put all the radiators on to full. The house warmed up very quickly, including the upstairs rooms. The water is also hot, but sometimes the pressure has been very low upstairs.

Now all we have to do is relax and lop around and get ready to leave. We went to the Roseraie last night. Nice meal cost 65 francs including a rather undistinguished Bergerac. We hope to go to the Sautet tonight, hopefully with the Smiths. (In the event it was full, so we went to the Soleil d'Or again.)

It is now 12.35. Glorious day. H. and J. are sitting by the pool. The last time I looked, the water temperature was 16 degrees.

M. Dartinset came over and gave us a bottle of home-made wine, which we shall take home probably. Jan arrived and we discussed future plans etc. I told him about the mower and gave him my letter with instructions. He will send me an estimate for doing the wall, which he will make at more than 55,000 francs. I should be able to get it from insurance, as it is not subsidence in the strict sense. Jan and M. D. both thought the idea of a drainage ditch was very good. It will protect the foot of the wall from wet, but M. D. did not think it would be necessary to rebuild the wall. Jan was not so sure. Neither am I. I would rather have it done properly.

Friday, 7 December 2001

A few notes more. The winter has started and we are all at home in Meopham. Mum is staying with us, following a fall down her stairs, which left her with a broken pelvis requiring hospital treatment. We have put a spare bed in the telephone room for her. Today we are going for lunch with Peter and Margaret[19] who have turned up trumps as they always do when something goes wrong (in this case my head).

I received estimates for the wall from M. Subresi and Jan and sent them both off to the insurance company. If they agree to pay, fine. If not I will pay. We have quite a lot of time, as M. Subresi is expecting to get the job done by Easter next year. Jan says he has cleaned up the garden by cutting down the tree by the pool and the cherry tree a bit further away. Both were nice trees, but they were in the wrong position – cutting them down should make it easier to keep the pool clean as well. Jan has also sawn up the cherry log left after the storm of December 1999.

I am improving slowly but steadily. Today is a good day and I am probably being too impatient in expecting to get better more quickly. I have to see M. Bullock next month for another scan and check-up, and I may then get my driving licence back. I am thinking about new cars – possibly a Peugeot 307.

* * *

Friday, 29 March 2002

We are down here for Easter with Jenny. She and Heather are downstairs doing some vigorous housework. I am here, slaving over a hot computer. It is quite cold, because there is a very strong easterly wind blowing, but basically it is very good weather. The house as usual was in very good condition. Some fouine droppings on the stairs to the basement room and also in our bathroom. Don't know how they got there. M. Subresi of Renomat has mended the kitchen corner. I must remember to pay him the balance. I shall have to go to see him, since I can't remember how much it is.

The garden is looking good. Needs a bit of a mow, but in general not too much attention required. We are both very pleased. Heather has found where the fouines get in. There is a big hole under the sink in the bathroom. We shall have to block it up.

I have found the weather forecast for Perigueux. It is under CompuServe, but actually links to the weather.com.uk. Very easy and gives a long, ten-day forecast. How accurate this is I don't know. I phoned Mum to say we had arrived. We have to go over to see the Dartinsets soon and then to give Sylvie her present. It is a drawing of the house that I did two years ago, before my Big Op. The house is warming up. The upstairs radiators didn't work at first but seem to be okay now – the tops are not very warm. Jenny says that means there is an airlock.

Saturday, 30 March 2002

Another fine day. Still rather a chilly wind, but we had lunch outside by the pool. Then I got the mower started (I had to charge the battery up) and then had a problem, because both front tyres were deflated. We took them to the Husqvarna place on the N89. The lady there could have pumped them up, but one of the nozzles had got lost inside the tyres when it went down so she had to wait for the mechanic. We have to get a plumber in because we have a bad leak in the bathroom tap. Sylvie came over this morning. She is starting a two-year hairdressing apprenticeship in Perigueux when she leaves school in July. She is looking forward to it. The Smiths arrived yesterday in their brand new Jaguar and we saw Roger Brière this morning. He has so much work on that they didn't have time to go to the Pyrenées.

Sunday, 31 March 2002

Quite warm, mainly because there is no wind. But we had lunch indoors, because it wasn't that warm. I got up late, feeling a bit unsteady. Nobody feels like doing very much. We have heard the cuckoo singing and making holes in trees and Heather says she saw it when she and Jenny went to get the paper this morning. I have to take one of the front wheels of the mower into the Husqvarna place on Tuesday morning because the mechanic could only pump up one of them. Doesn't matter much because we still have plenty of time. The garden looks very nice, and it is better without the tree by the pool. We shall have to plant some shrubs at the bottom to give more protection – for the plants, not us.

Monday, 1 April 2002

Another very bright but rather chilly morning. It is now 9.45am – the clocks have changed twice since we arrived in France, the last time being on Sunday. It is a bank holiday here as well. We lit the fire in the kitchen and it seems to burn well and the smoke has not really come into the room. We don't know quite why. The little pillar-box in the village has gone – taken away last year as an economy measure, I suppose. That means we have to go to Thenon to post our cards. I've tried to use the Internet a few times, but it is difficult getting a connection and then keeping one.

Wednesday, 3 April 2002

Today it has been raining for most of the time. Not heavy rain, but very persistent. We went to Jardiland and M. Bricolage, where I bought some O rings for the upstairs tap. I hope they are the right size. There are thousands of them. I have to go to see Douglas and tell him what I have done, so he can come and help me fix it. We also have to go and pick up the wheel of the mower, although I don't suppose I shall be able to use it until the weekend, because it will probably rain tomorrow morning as well. We ate in last night and I was sick. I can't hold my food down very well these days, and it can be embarrassing, especially when we go out for a meal. It also leaves me feeling hungry. But as soon as I have been sick I feel well again. Another visit to the doctor when I get home. M. Lespinasse and one of his men came today to do some small electrical jobs, including the lights in the utility room and the one over the washbasin upstairs... He also fitted a light in the downstairs shower. It all looks very much better and I am glad we had it done. I phoned M. Martinez about fixing the leaking tap, but he is in hospital for an operation on his leg. We bought a photinia or something at Jardiland. The idea is to put it at the base of bank by the pool to give the plant on the bank some shelter from the wind.

We have lit the kitchen fire a few times. It doesn't smoke very much and certainly makes that room very comfortable. We sit and look at the flames. That's what people did before they had televisions.

The grass is now growing very quickly and the lawn badly needs a mow. A few days of sunshine and a bit of rain is just what it likes.

Friday, 5 April 2002

Overcast, a bit of light drizzle this morning, but not so bad that we could not do some gardening. We planted two Clematis montanas, one by a tree in the wood and one by the little house on the prairie. Then we put in another plant at the bottom of the bank by the pool near where the tree used to be that we had cut down. It was quite tiring. I have been a bit unsteady today and Heather's aches and pains have been troubling. We had soup and cheese for lunch and that made her feel a lot better. We got some petrol this morning. Paid by card. The French don't seem to have any trouble with the euro and no one seems to be crying for the lost franc. I think it changed its value so many times that it had ceased to have any strong patriotic symbolism. They call the fractions of the euro, centimes, just like the franc, and seem just as anxious to get hold of change. At least the shopkeepers do. Many people pay for things by handing over a note and letting the shop sort it out. Tonight we are going to the Mule Blanche with Douglas and Shirley, as this is their last day. They came last night for an aperitif and Jan happened to call in while they were here. It was all very pleasant. Jan said he and his wife would come over some time. It will be nice to meet her.

March/April 2002

Heather

We came down with Jenny doing all of the driving and made excellent time, arriving at 5.30 to find the house looking good. The wall has been totally repaired, both inside and out and the front door and shutters all fit beautifully now. The kitchen was covered in cement dust but Jen and I cleaned it up on Good Friday. The garden looks lovely with the kerria being the best I've seen it and the japonicas all in bloom. Jan has chopped the old ash tree down beside the pool and the view is now uninterrupted. I think the pool will benefit from the lack of leaves there too. We had our first meal on arrival at le Orée du Bois, and it was very good. We cooked in most of the holiday, and found that the fire in the kitchen no longer smokes, so every evening we spent in we lit it, which made the kitchen a much warmer and more welcoming room to be in. We ate at the Mule Blanche with the Smiths but I found the food disappointing. However, Jan told us about Le Croquant in Fanlac and we went there on our last Sunday for lunch. It was excellent and we shall be going there again. It only opens on Sundays for lunch out of season, but during July/August it is open daily, so it is a good addition to our repertoire.

We visited Sergeac and met the new people in our old cottage, who seemed to be very nice. Madame and Claude seem to have aged but are still going strong, and the village looked just as it always does. Our last meal out was at Le Sautet, but was highly priced and of poor value we all thought. However, I had a rumtoff type of fruit and ice-cream dessert, which was delicious, and I am determined to do a rumtoff again at home this year.

The holiday passed all too quickly but we all enjoyed it I think, and Roger seems to be much more alert now. He had a gamma knife treatment at the end of January, to get rid of the remaining parts of the tumour and that seems to have gone very well. He is still not allowed to drive yet, hence Jenny doing so much this holiday, but we have hopes that he will soon be able to drive again. We plan to go to France again for the whole of August but think we may not get time to go before that as treatment, scans etc. are filling up our diary of events. We may be able to take a short break somewhere in England this spring.

Wednesday, 10 April 2002

We came home yesterday in fine style. Jenny drove. We were back by late afternoon, but decided to pick up the cats today – Heather is out doing that now while I am waiting for the electricity board to come and take away the unwanted meter. When we left it was cold and raining, but as we got past Limoges the weather and improved all the way to Calais, when it became overcast again. We went to the club lounge and had coffee and afternoon tea.

I have decided to get together a tool kit, rather like Douglas's. I could carry it in the car and would therefore have it here and there as well. Then I could do various simple jobs, like plumbing. Before we left I told Jan about then debroussailleuse (we couldn't get it to start). This may be partly due to the fact that I put lead-free petrol in instead of a mixture (which I have a can of). He said he will fix it. Just put some mixture on the spark plug (or was it the carburettor?), he said.

Thursday, 18 April 2002

We are planning to go back for August, Christopher and Julie[20] say they are still hoping to come over, but even if they don't we are looking forward to a good time. I hope I will be able to drive then. It is very inconvenient without the car and especially so now that I am feeling more active, even though my balance is still poor. I phoned M. Bullock's secretary to say that the DVLA have written to me to say they have been trying to get some response from him about my condition and she said she would look into it. I am planning to get a new car, when I get the go-ahead to drive again. Probably a Peugeot 307.

Saturday, 20 April 2002

The traditional way of life is dying here in rural France, just as it is in southeast England. The Dartinset family still do things the way they have been done probably for decades, but they say that the young people don't copy them. They prefer to go to the supermarket. Mme Dartinset still makes and tins her own pâté and rillette, while a few years ago Jean-Paul came over with a dustbin liner full of cêpes, which he had picked on their land. I cooked them and tried to preserve them, but they didn't taste very good when we got home. The trouble was we were leaving the next morning and couldn't do much with it. M. Dartinset also makes his own wine. He has a small vineyard on the left as you take the small road to Fossemagne. One day he and his friends had the vendange. They brought all the grapes to the farm and put them in a big vat, which then pressed the grapes. They then bottled the wine. I don't know what it tasted like, but when we were in Sergeac a man came to mend the lauze roof of the house next door. I gave him water etc. (it was very hot) and he gave me a bottle of his home-made wine. It was almost undrinkable. The moral is if you are thirsty, buy your wine in a shop.

Mme Dartinset can also remember the burning of Rouffignac by the Das Reich Division. She could see the flames from her home, which was the one where Jean-Paul lives now. The market at Thenon has shrunk over the years and last year I remember reading about how local markets are under threat. I can well believe that the market traders don't like the hard work involved in moving every night, setting up their stalls and so on, especially if the rewards are not very great.

I remember reading in the *Sud-Ouest* some time ago that it takes about 600 people (or maybe more) to maintain a baker's shop. That is one reason why the French government has always been so keen on maintaining local agriculture and industry. If the farms die, the villages die. If the villages die, the whole area becomes a desert. Once the villages reach a critical point they can no longer be sustained. The local schools close, people move away, there is nothing for the young people to do. And the towns and cities are so far apart that they cannot maintain a network of dormitory villages, as they do in England. We drove through the southern Massif Central some years ago. It was full of empty villages and crumbling walls (this was the area just north of Roquefort). France is so big that the population is spread very thin. In Dordogne most people are well aware of the benefits foreigners like us bring. Without us, half the houses would be abandoned.

Thursday, 1 August 2002

Back again, this time for the rest of the month. We came in our new Peugeot 307 automatic, which we both like very much. Heather did most of the driving, because the DVLA told me a few weeks ago that I could not drive until September, a year after the operation. This is a bore. We tried to avoid Paris and to come down in easy stages. This didn't work out too well. I tried to cross the Seine around Mantes, but this brought us very close to Paris, which Heather didn't want to go near. Eventually, we managed to cross the river and after that made our way to Orleans, where we planned to stay at a hotel we stayed at a few years ago. Of course, we couldn't find it, so we ended up at a Campanile at La Source, south of the city. It was quite adequate and we both slept like logs. The total bill came to 124.50 euros, including 53 for the room and 12 for breakfast. The evening meal was 31.

The next day, we kept on going to Brive and should have been at Jarripigier by early afternoon. Then we hit a huge traffic jam near Terrasson and had to dodge around that. Still, we arrived about an hour late. It was very hot, well, just hot, I suppose. Today it is cooler, quite a lot of cloud but so far (3.30) no rain. The forecast for the next three days is rain according to AOL.

Talking of which, I have spent two days trying to install AOL. I managed it today, so we can now get emails from home. Jenny thinks she will be able to come – she left her passport at home, but is asking a friend to get it for her.

The house is in very good shape. Jan was cutting the lawn when we arrived. But the plants all seem healthy, except for a small elm tree north of the large hazel, which has died in the last two months, presumably of Dutch elm disease. The Grahams were here in July and seem to have loved it. They are related to Jan's wife.

Friday, 2 August 2002

A lovely day. Sunny, warm, not too windy. We hoovered the pool in the morning and it is coming up very well. M. Courcaud had to empty it and then fill it again, so the water bill will be quite high for this quarter. Still, it is the first time in eight years so we can't complain too much. We still don't know how the thing got damaged, but the main thing is it now seems to be working properly again. We also had a slight problem with the washing machine, which was full or partly full of water. Heather cleaned the filter this morning. It was completely bunged up and this must have stopped the water escaping. We cleaned it and now it works properly again. We had a late breakfast by the pool, which was very pleasant. I might go for a swim later, like when I have finished this, but I shall probably chicken out. Heather is much braver than I am when it comes to swimming.

I cleaned out the cave this morning, or started it. I took a big barrow load of rubbish to the wheely bin, including old parasols and other junk. It has cleared a lot of room and we have unearthed a few treasures, for example, an old drill that Mel must have left there. I shall do some more when I am feeling stronger.

Saturday, 3 August 2002

Rather dull but pleasant. We had breakfast and then went off to M. Bricolage, which has moved to a bigger store in the same complex, then Jardiland and Leclerc. We bought a thermometer for the pool – the old one is broken – some plants, some meat for lunch tomorrow and one or two other bits and pieces. We were going to have lunch in Perigueux but it was rather early so went to Montignac and had lunch at the Hotel de la Grotte, which is opposite the turning for Lascaux. We had the 16 euro menu and the total bill with coffee was 35.50. It is a nice place, but not many people there. It amuses Heather because it tries hard but doesn't quite make it: the chandeliers have bulbs that don't work and the carpets are all faded. We had the Regourdou lunch: A salad and duck starter, then confit and cheese. Then home. The pool temperature is 24 degrees, a bit chilly but okay. The outside temperature is about the same.

M. Courcaud came over yesterday. I paid him and M. Cestari for the work they have done – about 420 euros each. The mystery about what happened to the control panel remains. When M. C. arrived the wiring had all been pulled out and it looked as though it was done on purpose. But the cave door was locked and there was no other sign of damage. I told him to leave the summer cover out this winter. It has a cover over it and it is a bit difficult getting it into the cave. When it is there it blocks up the entrance.

Sunday, 4 August 2002

Another dull but not cold day. Some rain earlier and a patch of sun, but not enough to get excited about. This computer needs a new mouse. We lit the bonfire last night and it was still going, or smouldering, this morning. Heather has done a lot of pruning and cutting back of shrubs. This all burnt very quickly and easily but the green stuff and leaves that were covered in mould and earth did not. Still, we got rid of an awful lot of rubbish and made lots of smoke. Some of the plants are doing very well. The abelia on the bank by the pool is in flower and the japonica at the back of the pool is quite rampant. Some of the roses have flowered and are ready to flower again, so Heather dead-headed them to give them some encouragement. We wrestled with the Flymo yesterday. It will be very useful for cutting the bank by the pool and in the japonica and all it needs is a new plug – the existing one does not stay in. We'll get one tomorrow, or next time we are near a shop that sells such things. I also need some music. I sorted some out at home but forgot to bring it. There should be a shop in Perigueux where I can get some. Good for practice. A month is a long time not to play. I have set up the keyboard, but Heather suggests putting her dressing table in the PC room for use as a piano table. We'll try. It could work. Today we had roast turkey from Leclerc. Quite nice. With salad and roast potatoes. We bought some strawberry tarts for tea, so that is something to look forward to. I rang Viv but she wasn't in. Her house sale seems to have fallen through because there is a survey problem with the wall at the bottom on the garden.

Monday, 5 August 2002

Heather

Yesterday we both saw a huge heron flying out from the wood and over towards the pond at the back of the Dartinsets. I had heard it squawking in the wood for ages and thought it was simply jays or magpies; but no, a grey heron, identified from the book. Later yesterday I saw a pair of treecreepers on the plum tree by the front edge of our little wood. I was searching for the bird(s) that are knocking on the wood of the dead oak that marks the boundary of our land but I have never managed to get close enough to see them. I feel that they are not woodpeckers, as they don't knock fast enough, so I think they must be thrushes or blackbirds in search of the insects inside the dead tree. While I have been dead-heading and pruning like mad, I have seen hordes of dark brown, hairy caterpillars and a few large chestnut-coloured hairy ones with bright orange dots on their sides but I can't identify them from the insect book. Swallows dive-bombed our pool yesterday and there are loads of house martins zooming about after the insects.

Monday, 5 August 2002

The weather today was pleasant. A bit of rain perhaps, but not much. Mostly cloudy, but some sun in the evening. We got the Flymo going, but it needs a new plug really. I went to the hardware shop in the morning, but when I went back in the afternoon it was closed. Jan came round in the afternoon. He got the strimmer working (I had it on stop). I showed him how to work the hoover in the pool. The attachment has broken and it needs a new piece, like a long screw, but as the hardware shop was shut it will have to wait until tomorrow, which is market day. I also need some contact lens stuff. We ate in tonight (cold meat, mashed potato and soup). We plan to go out tomorrow night. We had a message from Jenny to say her passport should arrive tomorrow and then she will look into how to get here.

Tuesday, 6 August 2002

Cloudy, some showers, not much sun, but quite warm. Forecast not too good. We went to the market today. We are going out this evening, so we did not buy much food. The market was quite busy. We saw most of the Dartinsets there, including Sylvie, who now has a silver ornament in her nose. I wanted to buy some contact lens solution, but the queue was too long. Bought bread and paper. More stalls than usual, including two selling fish. The estate agent at the bottom, which was always full of very old, faded photographs of very old faded houses has now been taken over by Mobiliers de France, who have also taken over Monsieur Mons' shop in Montignac. They seem to be expanding quite fast.

I managed to fix the pool vacuum – it needed a long metal piece, which I found. I also fixed the electric plug on the Flymo. The new plug is simpler than the one I tried yesterday but the connections for the wire are complicated and not very effective. I think it will hold but I am not sure. If it doesn't work, I know what is wrong.

The elm north of the hazel has died (Dutch elm).

The bonfire finally went out today, or during the night, but we have piled it high with more cuttings. Heather is cutting everything back hard, because otherwise the whole garden looks overgrown. It is beginning to look very nice. Once we have finished burning things we will dump the remains of the tree stump in the wood, level off the bonfire and use the earth and ashes to level off holes and hollows around the garden. We might put some grass seed down, but I think the scar of the fire will soon heal. Then we will start a new compost heap at the end of the white alley and eventually move the existing compost heap up there. The existing one is quite effective, but it is very unsightly. We want a long sweep of lawn running the full length of the garden. Wrote a few cards today.

I have read *Rebecca's Tale* by Sally Beauman, who is a very good and, I think, rather under-rated novelist (mostly romantic, women's stories, but well told), and *Marie Antoinette*. The sun is coming out, probably only for a few moments, so I shall stop now and go into the garden.

We went to the Mule Blanche for dinner and ate outside on the terrace. The wisteria has grown enormously and it was very nice. Total bill 46 euros, including half a bottle of Tiregand, and two bachelier menus.

Wednesday, 7 August 2002

Very warm now (1.45pm) and sunny. The forecast says this will be the warmest day of the week. The *Sud-Ouest* has a story about the lost summer. Where is the sunshine and why has it disappeared? The reason, it seems, is that there is an anticyclone over the Azores which is dominating weather here (and also in Britain, I suspect). July was a dead loss from the point of view of sunshine. About the worst year since 1958 apparently. August doesn't seem to be much better. The trouble is also that there is not much rain, so the farmers are being doubly hit. The wine growers say it is not too bad, but they would like some sun this month. The campsites are in trouble and in some places holiday takings are down 30%. The bars in town are okay. People don't go to the beach when the weather is bad, they go out for a drink near home.

We did a bit more clearing up and cleaned the pool and then sat down. Heather is making teddy bears and I have been reading about the Cathars. Tomorrow night is supposed to be the night of the stars, with a great display, all visible. But I think we shall have the clouds in the way. I need a small screwdriver to bleed the radiators upstairs. I can't get the ordinary ones in the space. A job for M. Bricolage at some stage.

Jan, Mary and her brother-in-law Robert came round for an aperitif. Nice to meet them. They were going to Chez Maria for dinner – we thought it might be closed, but they said no. But they agreed that Isabelle's departure was a big blow.

Friday, 9 August 2002

Today it is raining. Quite heavy rain, too. The sky is grey, with no hint of *eclaircies* (sunny periods) and it is forecast to continue until lunchtime. We think we will go to Terrasson this afternoon, partly because it is a day out and partly because we need some secateurs (the existing ones have broken), some easy chairs and a pump for lilos, etc. The weather is terrible all over Europe, so we are not alone. Nevertheless, it would be nice to have a hot day for a change. The pool is around 24 degrees, a bit cold for swimming in. The outside temperature when we went to Thenon this morning was 14 degrees. We bought some artichokes for lunch and plan to have onion soup and prawns this evening. I think I might light the living room fire if we are staying in. Yesterday I mowed the lawn. I had to fill the petrol tank twice and still didn't finish it all. But I began another grass-cutting pile at the end of the white alley. The rain today means that we can't light the bonfire. It is getting bigger all the time as we cut back shrubs and other scrub. Jenny has worked out a fiendishly complicated route here, which means she will arrive late at night. Probably coming on the 22nd.

Saturday, 10 August 2002

Another unsettled day. We decided to go to Perigueux in the morning, to take advantage of the weather, but the town was full, we couldn't park, so we came home. We are trying to get some recliners and other easy chairs because the old ones have all broken but have had no luck so far. We have been to M. Bricolage, Jardiland, Leclerc and Conforama. We saw Roger Brière in Thenon yesterday. They are going to Dax tomorrow to take the waters. This is for the benefit of his knees, which are very painful. He manages to keep cheerful, despite it all.

It is now 2.35pm and quite sunny. But there are lots of cloud around. Still, it is better than yesterday, when it rained more or less all day. Lots in the paper about the bad weather, with tourists being interviewed about whether they will come again next year. Most said yes. Jenny says she will be coming on 20 August. We think she should hire a car and come here, rather than try to meet us in Perigueux. For one thing she knows the way here and also we have no idea when she will arrive. The train journey was too complicated and there was always the risk that something would go wrong. We tried our mobile phones yesterday, not very successfully, but we did manage to establish that I have no money left to make calls!

Sunday, 11 August 2002

Not very nice. Overcast, rainy at times. Last night was supposed to be the night of the stars, with millions of stars on display. We couldn't see anything for the clouds. (**Heather:** I did see the stars when I looked out before I went to bed and they looked spectacular. There are still three more nights to go so I may see more of them. How clear the sky is here with such little pollution.) Still, the meteo promises good August weather starting on Tuesday (if you believe Meteo de

France, as the *Sud-Ouest* says cynically). We bought bread and the paper and plan to eat in today. We cut back the fig, which grows rampantly every year, and then cleaned the pool. We will have to rearrange the bonfire and I put some of the fig green stuff up in the corner, out of the way. There was a *brocante* (antiques) fair in Thenon today. I saw a Brown Bess musket from the Tower of London that we saw in Montignac last week. Mostly a lot of old tat, but some nice things. We got up late – about ten. We seem to get up later each day. We were getting up at seven or eight last week, but now it is nine or ten, although Heather tends to get up earlier than me.

Monday, 12 August 2002

Cloudy, cold – but the meteo promises that the good weather will start tomorrow and by the end of the week it will be very hot. The paper today is full of doom and gloom about the weather, because there is not enough sun for the tourists and not enough rain for the farmers. Yesterday we had a phone call from Alex Roch, inviting us for lunch on Tuesday (i.e. tomorrow). That will be a nice day out, especially if the sun shines. We are still looking for some comfortable poolside chairs, but so far without much luck. We saw a few at the Intermarché in Montignac today but they weren't quite right. I thought I also saw Maia, the daughter of the Mailly family from Marseille who come to Sergeac in the summer. But she didn't see us and I didn't speak. We hope to go to Sergeac on Wednesday for a pétanque competition. I imagine Claude will be playing. Heather is painting the door from the kitchen to the annex, the aim being to brighten it up and eventually paint over the dark brown wood. A very good idea.

Wednesday, 14 August 2002

At last, good weather. It began yesterday, hot and sunny all day long. We went over to Brâ to see Edward and Alex Roch. Another couple called Bobby and Margaret, who have a house in Lot et Garonne, were there. She is the painter and he collects old cameras. We had a lovely lunch, with roast chicken, walked around the garden and looked at the pool. We left at about 4.30 and got home about 7.15, having tried to find some interesting routes, but only getting tired.

Today the sun is still shining and it is expected to go on until Saturday, when we shall probably get thunder.

We got up at about 8am and then went to get petrol and bread. We plan to do nothing much today. After our long trip yesterday we need to rest. We cleaned the pool – Edward has had trouble with his pool this year – and Heather is trimming back some shrubs. We plan a bonfire this afternoon, when the cuttings should have dried up a bit. I plan to mow the lawn again today – the grass grows quite fast, partly because we have had rain.

Thursday, 15 August 2002

Today is a public holiday in France and nothing much seems to be happening anywhere. This is just as well, because we were a little fragile and spent the whole day sitting around and not doing much at all. I used the hammock, which is very pleasant. The pool temperature went up to 25 degrees in the sun and generally it has been a perfect day, hot and sunny, but pleasant enough in the shade, with just a hint of wind from the west. The garden is looking quite good now. Most of the shrubs we planted are thriving and the wood is very pleasant. I went through it with the mower the other day and it is now quite open and accessible. The lawn area is huge. It takes about two hours to cut it and I would not like to do it with an ordinary push mower. Tomorrow we plan to go looking for deckchairs and may have food out as well. Sarlat is a possibility. We were going to do this today, followed by a visit to a pétanque competition at Sergeac, but we didn't get round to it and anyway the shops would probably all have been closed.

Friday, 16 August 2002

Also part of the long holiday weekend: glorious weather. We went to Perigueux, partly to look for chairs and eventually we found one in a shop in the old town. Unfortunately, they only had the one, so we bought it for 27.25. We had a coffee and wandered around and then we decided to go to the Ecluse for lunch. This is where we stayed after Heather's operation in 1998. It was lovely and seems to be doing well; the receptionist was telling someone on the phone that they were fully booked up for tonight and it didn't look too good for the next day either. We had the menu of the day for 18 euros. Soup of the day (vegetable), pâté or crudités, magret of duck or fish, ice cream and coffee. It was very good, with excellent service. The total bill was 38.30 euros, or 251.23 francs. Very elegant setting, some people were playing with their dog in the river. It is so shallow the dog could walk more than halfway over. Then we came home and did a bit of gardening and resting. The bonfire site is almost cleared now. We shall go over it with the Flymo and then the mower. The pool has reached 26 degrees. I was almost tempted today.

Sunday, 18 August 2002

Hot and sunny, just like Saturday. Yesterday we just pottered around. Then we went to Jardiland to get some pool things, including something to lower the pH because the level was too high. We came back and Jean-Paul and Sylvie came over to tell us that she had used the pool. We knew this because there were footprints on the patio and the chair was in the shade so her grandfather could watch (she likes this). That evening she and some friends had a party outside her grandparents' house. It went on all night and they made a great deal of noise, just having fun – talking, squealing and so on. It was all very innocent, but in the morning her parents made them go round apologising to people. Today we are going to Fanlac for lunch. I booked a table yesterday. I went swimming on Saturday afternoon. The temperature was about 26 – 27 degrees. Lovely.

I did the drive with Round Up this morning, but will have to go over it again. I don't think the concentration was strong enough. The Hozelock spray works very well.

Monday, 19 August 2002

Dull and overcast, with morning mist. The forecast is for heavy, dull weather with some thunderstorms likely. That seems very possible, but it should brighten up after a few days. Tomorrow should see lots of rain. We can't complain and I know the farmers would like to see some. Today we went to the Shopi at Rouffignac. It is bigger than the Huit à 8 and has a better selection. We did quite a big shop and are still hoping that Jenny will come, perhaps tomorrow, but we haven't heard anything.

Heather has painted the cupboards in the kitchen, a creamy colour that certainly brightens up the whole room. A very good idea. I charged up the battery in the mower (it wasn't very flat) and was quite pleased with that because I wasn't sure that I could get the cover off. Fortunately, it was not too difficult – a question of using the right tool. This is the fourth smallest of the reverse Allen keys, and I have now marked it with paint for future reference. Then I got the debroussailleuse going. The secret is to use gloves, as the pull can make the fingers quite sore. I pumped it up and put the choke on but I think this flooded the engine. So I put the choke off and it started almost at once. The engine gets very hot and you have to make sure you don't burn your arm.

The pool temperature was 26 degrees.

Tuesday, 20 August 2002

A complete change. When we woke up it was pouring with rain and there was lots of thunder about, not overhead, just circling round us. By late morning the thunder had gone and the rain stopped and the forecast is for better weather this afternoon.

Jenny has decided not to come. She would not get to St Malo until 12.30, by which time the car hire place would be closed for lunch. She would not make it down here until very late, so it is not worthwhile. We have to find some indoor things to do. Heather will continue painting units in the kitchen. It looks much better with them being a light colour. We also have some pictures to put up.

We spent a lot of yesterday cleaning the pool, from inside. I stood on the vacuum head and sort of scootered it round the bottom and Heather scrubbed at it with the brush on the shortest pole. It worked and the pool looks better for it. As it is raining and not very nice I doubt if we will use it today.

Thursday, 22 August 2002

Today started quite fresh, with a mackerel sky and little sun. But the sun came out by mid-morning and it looks like being another hot sunny day. The forecast is not quite so rosy, but who can tell?

We went to Sergeac to see the Deljarrys and also the Campbells, who bought Nita's house. They are going home today. Mme. D. looked quite a bit older and rather frail, but Claude hasn't changed.

He came third in the Sergeac pétanque competition on 15 August. He said forty-eight teams took part.

Then we went on to the garden of Marqueyssac, near Vezac, on the Dordogne. A lovely castle, with a wonderful position high on a cliff top facing Castelnaud and with a good view of Beynac and, around the other way, of la Roque-Gageac and Domme in the distance on the other side of the river. A feature of the garden, which must be at least a mile long, is its topiary – 150,000 boxes, all neatly clipped. It was a hot day and the garden takes a lot of walking, but there is a very nice café there and a *caleche* (a horse drawn carriage) gives lifts to people who don't have any energy left to walk. We were very impressed. Worth a visit for those new to the area and rather like Eyrignac in a way. A bonus is that you can wander around; you don't have to wait for an organised visit. We only walked around the topiary section, and left the long walk to other people. Home just after 6pm.

Friday, 23 August 2002

A dull day with some rain and not very warm. The good weather seems to have deserted us, at least for the time being. We didn't feel like doing things in the garden or the house, so we went to Shopi for our shopping and then went off again, first to Cubjac, which was dull, rather run down and closed for lunch, and then on to Hautefort, the idea being to have lunch there. We did. We ate at Le Mediéval, which is on the main square. We ate outside, under the shade of a huge tree. Not very warm. It cost 23.30 euros for two and was okay (we both had magret) but not wonderful. Then it started to rain quite hard, so we gave up our walk around the old town and came home. It is quite good going out for lunch. It makes a break, especially when the weather isn't very good, enables us to sightsee, and then gives us the rest of the day for chores. We also went à la carte rather than picking a menu. This means we can have a smaller meal which suits us in the middle of the day. Usually a glass or two of wine is plenty and it means we can still do things in the afternoon. We shall probably go for lunch on Sunday, possible to the Soleil d'Or.

I started chopping up logs this morning, but the axe is really too small and took forever just to chop up one. I need a bigger axe.

Heather

The garden we visited yesterday was special and the topiary cut in those cloud formations rather than geometric shapes. I can't think how we have never been there before as it is very well established and is called a parc rather than a jardin. Also on the blurb that you are given everywhere, I saw that the Commanderie at Comargue is now open to the public, with a lot about the finding of the hidden village etc. In one way it is good that it is open once more, but I still feel that it was an impressive secret place and should perhaps have remained so. The forecast is not too good for the rest of our stay, although, the weather has usually been better for us than the forecast anyway, so we may be lucky. We both have plenty of things to do around the house and garden anyway so I doubt that any weather will spoil the holiday for us now.

We cleaned the pool and did other things when we came back from Hautefort. The rain didn't amount to much and it stopped in the afternoon anyway. We noticed that the pool looked a little bit green and milky so we assumed that it was about to get covered in algae. I found some Chlore Lent and I put in two round disks and then we went to the new Bricomarché shop by Shopi in Rouffignac and I bought five litres of anti-algae liquid. We shall leave the filter on overnight with the chlorine in and then I shall add some algaecide tomorrow if necessary. Whether we need it or not, it is useful to have it in reserve. If it does get worse I shall contact M. Courcaud, but I don't want to do that unless I have to, especially as it is now the weekend.

I found a few bills in my wallet which might be interesting.

> Hotel Royal Vezére, 22 August: 40 euros for lunch. This was about our first attempt at going à la carte. Pricey and the waiter was snooty, but it was a good meal. We had half a bottle of rosé, which cost 5.50.

> L'Ecluse, 16 August: 38.30 euros. Pricey, but very good service and food. We had two menus of the day at 18 euros each and a quarter bottle of rosé. They give the price in francs as well (251.23).

Hotel de la Grotte, 3 August: 35.50 euros. This included two 16 euro menus and a quarter carafe of red.

Mule Blanche, 4 August: 46 euros. This was for dinner – two Bachelier menus and a half bottle of Tiregand.

Hotel Campanile, Orleans La Source, 31 July: We stayed there on the way down. 124.50 euros. This included breakfast, dinner, wine, etc.

Saturday, 24 August 2002

We had a minor crisis yesterday: the pool started to go green. I had changed the filter bag and the old one was so filthy I doubt it had been doing any filtering for days. I put a new bag on and put the filter on but then Heather said it was looking green and although I said it wasn't, it was. We found some Chlore Lent capsules and I put two of those in and we went of to Bricomarché at Rouffignac to get some algaecide. We bought a 5 litre can. By the time we got home the water seemed to be improving, so we left the pump on all night and didn't put any algaecide in. By the morning it had been transformed. The water was clear and sparkling and whatever algae remained seemed to be dead. We changed the bag again and did more hoovering and the difference was even greater. We nipped the problem in the bud, I think. The moral is to change the bag at least once a week and to keep checking the water condition.

The weather today is perfect – sunny and clear – although the weather forecast was much more gloomy. We also put up a trellis by the pool gate for the wisteria to grow over. It is doing very well indeed and by next spring should have made a very pretty arch over the gate. We bought a log splitter and I started cutting up wood, but it is hard work.

Sunday, 25 August 2002

Dull, cloudy, some drizzle. The forecast is that it will stay like this, but we have had some lovely days and have got a lot of things done so we don't mind very much. We shall probably go home on Wednesday, taking three days. That will enable us to get back on Friday, in time to help Viv with her move.[21] We think we will get her a bottle of champagne to celebrate. Today we cleaned out the roof gutter: a few years ago it got blocked by a tile and that flooded the kitchen ceiling. I had to drill a hole to let the water out. The kitchen looks very impressive and much lighter. Heather is giving the woodwork an extra coat and then plans to varnish it. We are planning to eat at the Soleil d'Or today and there is also a market at Rouffignac we want to look at.

Lunch at the Soleil d'Or was very pleasant. We had the Losse menus and half a bottle of Chateau Calabre blanc. Total cost 67.70 euros. We collected up some dried kindling in the wood. It will be useful in the autumn. We are now thinking of painting the fireplace black.

The Round Up has worked on the drive. Most of the weeds have turned yellow and are looking very sorry for themselves.

Monday, 26 August 2002

Another wet, dull, rainy day. We have decided to start going home tomorrow. There is no real point in staying, especially as the weather forecast continues to be bad. Yesterday we went to Rouffignac where we saw Jan, Mary and their son Nick. Jan will come over later this afternoon to talk about future plans. On the way back from the Soleil d'Or we got held up at Bars by a *vide-grenier* and had to come back via the little lane. So we stopped and looked at the vide-grenier anyway. The usual collection of not very interesting stuff. At Rouffignac there was a market and we bought some jam for Mum.

I have just put up some pictures in the kitchen and in the upstairs study-bedroom. We think we will make more of this room as it is one of the best in the house and the downstairs room is still dark and a bit damp. We will probably make it into a common room and use it as a store for garden furniture, etc. I put the heating on when we came back from getting the bread and paper today. It is not really cold, just miserable. We think we might go to Maria's tonight.

Heather

I have at last managed to identify the birds I see on the tree trunks as nuthatches and not treecreepers as I at first thought. The birds knocking at the dead tree are, after all, woodpeckers but probably young green ones and I found the sweetest little wren's nest in the hawthorn by the pool. All of the nestlings in the laurel – blackbird and robin – have now flown. We think we will start for home tomorrow after all as the weather is not good and Viv will probably be grateful for extra hands/bodies to help in these last stages of her move. It has been a good holiday, very restful and quiet, and the poor weather this summer hasn't really bothered us too much. As it has turned out Jen's decision not to come was probably a wise one as the weather forecast does not look good for the rest of the week, and it does free us to go home as and when we wish. We already know that we shall be returning fairly shortly anyway and it only remains to see for just how long we can stay then.

Saturday, 31 August 2002

We are now back home again. We left Le Jarripigier on Tuesday because the weather was lousy and the forecast was that it would stay that way until the end of the week. Also we wanted to be back to help Viv if necessary. We took three days for the journey. We stopped at Bourges the first night, at the Hotel d'Angleterre in the town centre, where they had a garage. Very useful, as even on-street parking has to be paid for there. Room was 74 euros, breakfast 17 euros and the garage 8.50 euros. We ate at another restaurant in town – there were hundreds of them – and were very impressed with the town. The restaurant was L'Ecrin du Lion d'Or and it cost 71.20 euros, including wine and coffee.

Then we drove on to Reims, which we also liked very much. We stayed at the Hotel Continental in the centre, parked in the underground car park by the hotel. We got there in the early afternoon, so we had time to walk around a bit. Total bill was 88 euros, including room, breakfast and parking. Lovely city. We ate at a small brasserie over the road. Very good; Heather had a salad and I had spaghetti bolognaise.

The next day was quite easy. We went up the motorway all the way to Calais and were home early in the afternoon, in time to go shopping, collect the cats etc. Motorway driving is boring, but efficient and fast. The other roads are okay, but you always have the problem of getting stuck behind lorries or caravans.

Our last meal at Chez Maria was very disappointing. We were the only ones there and they had to open up for us. The food was only adequate and the ambiance was totally missing. They lost a treasure when Isabelle left.

Sunday, 27 October 2002

It is now 1pm. French clocks have just gone back an hour, so we had longer in bed this morning, which was very nice as we had a long day yesterday. Up at 6am UK time, then the 8.45am ferry from Dover, because the 8.15 that we were booked on mysteriously failed to sail because of gales in the Channel. It was a bit rough but not too bad and no one was sick. We had priority booking and we left Calais at about 11am and got down here at about 7pm. It was a lovely sunny day, but windy in the north which meant we could not go all that fast. The car was fine and we averaged just over 27mpg. It is not as fast as the Rover, but you have to expect that with an automatic and we also had the air conditioning on all the way, which helps to account for the rather heavy fuel consumption. In the evening we went to the Périgord, by the river in Montignac, as the Orée du Bois was closed. We had a lovely meal, with a very pleasant waitress, and feel we should add it to our list. We ate so well we decided not to go for Sunday lunch today. We had a late breakfast instead.

We went to Thenon for bread and the paper, but the Huit à 8 was closed, so we went to the little shop up the road. Very good service. Later we went to Rouffignac, had a look at the market (rather bedraggled, because it was raining) went to the supermarket and then had a coffee. Back home and some housework.

The fouines have got into the bathroom, so Heather cleaned that up, and they also got into the kitchen. Apart from that, not too many problems. We have to block up various holes, but the radiators upstairs are now working (quite a relief). The main problem is that the crack in the kitchen wall has reappeared. I intend to go to Renomat tomorrow to get them to fix it. It was fine in August, but September has been very wet and this must have affected it. Since they were supposed to have cured the problem last time I think it is up to them to fix it this time. I also have to go to Sarlat to get a Carte Bleue[22] from the bank. Jenny says she will stay here and do things, like cleaning up the leaves that are on the drive way.

All in all, quite satisfactory. The house is lovely and warm and the central heating works a treat. The radiators heat up very quickly.

Heather

We heard an owl in the garden during the night and saw a hare on the way back from Montignac last night. All of the seedlings that we planted during the year seem to have survived thus far and we still have some figs on the tree. I am more than ever convinced now that the fig is in the wrong place and should be taken away. This would leave space for an extended patio by the living room doors, which would be of more use as the sun does get there during spring and autumn and early evenings. There would also be space underneath for dry storage too. The steps up need renovating anyway so the whole operation could be done in one go and make the living room entrance look very good. We think a new fig could be planted at the wood's edge and Mary says they only take two years to fruit anyway. We have also talked about clearing the yukka/berberis patch and planting two fruit trees against the end wall – a lovely sheltered place.

Monday, 28 October 2002

Heather and I went to Sarlat this morning to get my Carte Bleue and then we stopped at Renomat to tell them about the crack. They should come over during the week, but we don't think it is too serious. A lovely sunny day, but very misty to begin with. We are going to the Dartinsets for an aperitif at noon.

In the garden Jan has cleared the old compost heap and cut the laurels by the swimming pool. When they grow in the spring it will only be soft branches which we can cut easily. The patch where the bonfire was has now grassed over and the whole garden looks very nice, even though the lawn needs cutting. Still, that can probably wait until next year now. Jenny has been clearing leaves from the driveway, which looks good now. The hazelnuts have all gone, eaten by the squirrels.

Tuesday, 29 October 2002

Market day. Quite busy, but the big news from Thenon is the opening of a new Shopi at the top of the town, where the old garage used to be on the N89. It is quite big, much better then the old Huit à 8 and even the Shopi in Rouffignac. They sell meat and other things there, so we think it will be a place to make for in the future. The

Husqvarna shop on the N89 was also still open, but the Huit à 8 was closed, whether temporarily or not we don't know. We are going to eat in today. We went to the Orée du Bois yesterday and had a very good meal, but we were all tired and went to bed early. Another lovely day today. A bit warmer than yesterday. There is no doubt that it is cold here. I saw Roger Brière and he said it was cold. He went to Dax for a cure in the summer – hot baths, mud baths, massages, etc. We won't know for a year or more how effective it is but he thinks it has done him some good. He certainly looked good. Pauline retires in December and Jerome is now working for Jardiland in Toulouse. They are big, successful, but don't pay very well. Still it is better than running your own shop it seems.

Wednesday, 30 October 2002

Last night we ate in. We lit the kitchen fire and it burnt well. The ventilation hole under the window seems to have solved the smoke problem. M. Barbini came round in the afternoon to tell us we could pick the apples from the tree in the field (Pommes des Pommiers) at the bottom of our garden – he had lots of others and didn't want the bother of having to come over here to pick them. So we did that this morning. We got lots and lots of them. We shall probably take them back home with us and peel and make them into jam or something like that. We also collected some pine cones this morning. They burn very well and so we think we shall collect them when possible as fuel.

Friday, 1 November 2002

Toussaints, big French holiday weekend. Last night they celebrated Halloween, which seems to have caught on here more than in England. As the *Sud-Ouest* points out today, it is encouraged by shopkeepers looking for new markets.

Sylvie now has a new scooter. She brought it over to show us yesterday. It has a top speed of 45kph and no gears and because she is now 16 she doesn't need a licence or lessons. But she does need insurance and she is still waiting for that. She and her mother and the grandparents came over for an apero at noon yesterday.

Another nice day yesterday, despite the weather forecast, but today it is very misty. We are going to La Table du Terroir with Jan today for lunch. His wife Mary is in England this week, so he is on his own with the youngest daughter supposedly looking after him (he thinks he has cracked a rib).

We rather think that the Huit à 8 has closed down and moved up to the new Shopi. There is a sign outside saying it is now a Proxi, so maybe another chain has taken it over while the old shop has moved to bigger and better premises.

*   *   *

Sunday, 13 April 2003

We arrived yesterday. A fairly easy drive down. We got the 7.45am ferry and had a quick, easy journey until Paris when we hit some traffic jams, one caused by an accident, but others just by pressure of traffic. I think that the French holidays must have started at the same time as ours and everyone was going south from Paris on the same day. Anyway, we got here at about 6.15pm. That gave us time to unpack, make the beds and then go out for a meal. We went to the Mule Blanche, because the Orée du Bois was closed. We think it is closed on Saturdays, because most of its trade comes from lorry drivers who don't work on Saturdays.

This morning it was chilly at the start but fine and later the sun came out and it was wonderfully warm. We sat by the pool and had a coffee at lunchtime. Tonight we shall eat in because we brought some food with us and need to use that up. Heather and Jenny did lots of work in the house and got everything clean, while I mowed the lawn. The mower started first time. It ran out of petrol after a while, but I had some in the can and filled it up again. But I must remember to get some more petrol in a day or so. It grows so fast at this time of year. Jan has been and had already cut the lawn and done some weeding, but it needs to be done about twice a week. The lawn is now so big, because every time we cut the grass we seem to extend it a little. We are planning new treats for the house and garden. The fig tree has been cut down, as has the dead elm tree. Both are an improvement. We need a new fig for the garden and some more shrubs and flowers.

M. Subresi of Renomat has been and seems to have fixed the crack in the kitchen wall. No sign of any work (i.e. no dust) but the cracks have disappeared. Just two small hairline cracks on the inside, which don't look significant compared with the cracks that are everywhere in the house. The fouines have been back. They have been using the trap door as a toilet, so we need to do something about that. Also the tap in the bathroom runs very slowly so that the hot water heater doesn't come on. Maybe we need a plumber.

After I cut the lawn I put Round Up on the pathway. I shall do it again later, but it was not too bad at all, perhaps because I put Round Up down last year.

Anyway, the general feeling is that the house is in excellent condition and the weather is wonderful and looks set fair for the next week or so.

Monday, 14 April 2003

Not such a nice day. Cloudy and windy. We went to Desjoyaux in Terrasson to tell them to get the pool ready by 24 May but they asked me to phone M. Courcaud, who is doing the job. So I have that to do.

Last night Douglas and Shirley Smith arrived with their teacher friend Janie. They came over for an aperitif, as did Sylvie. She seemed quite happy to be amongst a lot of grown-ups all talking English, with me trying to translate. She is not at all shy. She is working as a waitress at the Relais des Chasseurs, which we don't go to because we got food poisoning there once, and when she leaves school in June she is going to a training school to learn the art of waitressing. They take that sort of things seriously in France. We gave the Dartinsets some Stilton and Sylvie some ear-rings for Easter. She said the Stilton was very good.

We had baked potatoes for lunch and this afternoon plan to go to Leclerc so I can get some money and then to Jardiland because we have to buy a fig to replace the one that was cut down by Jan. That move has turned out to be excellent – the kitchen is so much lighter as a result and this will be even more the case in the summer, when the leaves will be out.

Tuesday, 15 April 2003

Today is market day. We duly went in to Thenon and called on Roger Brière, who still has trouble with arthritis but is as cheerful as ever. Pauline is about to retire and they seem happy about that. We also saw M. Dartinset and the backview of M. Barbini. Not so busy as usual, perhaps because it is the holiday and people are away. Nevertheless, the familiar stalls were all there – the man selling live poultry down by the newsagent, the lady selling plants outside the hardware shop, the paella stall, the shoe stall and so on. Everyone was dressed up in their finest (i.e. with berets). We saw the Smiths' car there but not them. Tonight we are going with them to the Hotel de France at St Orse. Roger Brière says it is fine, good food; simple, and they don't smile a lot. We bought some plants and came back, had breakfast and Jenny and Heather are now outside planting them.

The weather is not so good as forecast. It is cloudy and windy and quite fresh at times. You need a coat or sweater on when you go out. I spoke to Jan yesterday and he said he had a lot of trouble starting our mower. He had to clean the spark plug and the filter. We also need a new air filter, he says. A chore for the near future. No wonder it started first time for me yesterday: Jan had done all the maintenance work.

Wednesday, 16 April 2003

A glorious day. Dry, sunny, temperature up in the 20s in the afternoon. There was still a bit of a chill in the morning but that was because the sky was so clear. Heather was not feeling too good (too much rich food) so we did very little and just had a light salad for lunch. Despite that, we went to Fanlac to check the Croquant restaurant and then to the Shopi at Rouffignac to buy some food and to the shop next door to get some stuff for the garden. We have been looking for a garden chair, but can't find the one we want. We might have to get it in England at this rate.

The countryside is looking lovely. Very green and the trees are all coming into leaf now, so there are lots of shades of green. But the good weather is causing some problems. According to a *Sud-Ouest* article headed "Ou sont les giboulées?" ("Where are the showers?"). There is plenty of water in the reservoirs, because of rain in the autumn and winter, and the snows will soon melt and provide more. But the farmers need rain for sowing their crops, because the land surface is very dry. The article suggests that global warming might be responsible.

Last night we went to the Hotel de France at St Orse with the Smiths. Quite adequate, standard Périgord food. We all had the 19 euro menus. Pâté with foie gras to start, then confit de canard. I think that is what made Heather ill, but she seems to be better now.

Today we spent the afternoon sitting by the pool. It was so hot nobody wanted to do anything more active. So we didn't.

Thursday, 17 April 2003

Another gorgeous morning, but rather cloudier than yesterday. Heather is much better. We don't plan to do very much all the same.

The paper today has a long article about anti-French feeling in the USA, with pictures of Americans pouring French wine away and switching to Italian or Australian. It could get serious if it continues. However, Europe seems to be getting together more and the EU has just welcomed more members from Eastern Europe.

Friday, 18 April 2003

Another glorious day, but likely to be the last one for a while as the weather is due to change, just in time for the Easter weekend.

The main development today has been with the central heating. It has packed up. We noticed something was wrong yesterday when it suddenly started making a noise – a rather alarming burring sound. I turned it off, put it on and the noise had gone. Anyway, I rang M. Aubin, who installed it in 1999, and left a message. Today I rang again and they say someone will come on Tuesday afternoon. I think the problem is the water pressure – there is not enough in the system, which is what made the noise. It should be at 1.5 bar, but ours is at about 0.5 and still going down. I tried adjusting the pressure by turning the blue *manette* (lever) at the back of the boiler, but it was already turned to the maximum and I couldn't move it any further. When I put on the hot water tap to do the washing up the heater didn't go on. That must be a safety reason, probably because of the low pressure. We haven't had it serviced since it was installed, so they will do that on Tuesday when they come. It is all a bit of a bore, but the Easter weekend is the problem. We can't expect them to come until it is over.

The heating came on this evening, but the water pressure is still low and we can't get hot water.

Saturday, 19 April 2003

Cold water shaving can be very painful. But we manage with kettles and things and fortunately the weather is still warm. I cut some logs yesterday, so we can use both fires if necessary. So even if the weather turns colder, as is forecast, we should still be warm enough in the house. The restaurant at Tursac was okay, but not very special. Not worth going all that distance for.

We have planted some more shrubs – some clematis to climb up the trees on the edge of the wood, some laurels in the white alley, a fig where the compost heap used to be. The bottom of the garden looks good now, with the compost heap gone and no trace of where the fire was lit around the roots of the old cherry tree. The remains of that are now on the edge of the wood.

Many trees and shrubs have come into flower, just in the last few days. The lime tree is now green – the leaves hardly showed a week ago. Some of our pale French lilies have come out, including another group just this morning. And even the shrubs that are in the shade are ready to burst into colour. The trouble is, most of them will be finished by the summer. So we need to plan our planting with different seasons in mind.

Sunday, 20 April 2003

For the first time we have seen some rain. This is exactly what was forecast, so we can't complain. It seems as though the next week will also be unsettled, with steady rain on Friday and Saturday. Still, we have had a wonderful week so we are not complaining.

Jan came over this morning. It is good having them here, keeping an eye on things for us. I told him about the water and he said it could be because the pipes have furred up with limescale. We will find out on Tuesday when the man comes.

The flowers and leaves are enjoying the moisture. Everything looks green and verdant and Jan said that the weather has been exceptionally warm here, as it has at home. We are going for lunch today to the Croquant at Fanlac. We have been before and liked it. Yesterday I did Douglas's lawn again and was hoping to do ours today. But it is now too wet. I also need to go to the Honda place in Perigueux to get a new air filter – the existing one is so dirty, Jan says, that it needs to be replaced. The mower certainly shoots out a lot of dirty black smoke when it starts. Maybe that is the reason.

It is now 5.10pm. We went to lunch at Fanlac and had a huge meal for 19.50 euros. Soup to start, then rillettes, then omelette or chicken, then confit of pork or chicken, then cheese, then crêpes. It was very good. The restaurant was full of mainly local families. The service was very good too – the waitress coped with everyone without fuss or mistakes either. We lit both fires, as it was chilly. Jenny insisted on sitting in front of the kitchen fire, even though the other one is much more efficient and the room is more comfortable.

Monday, 21 April 2003

Got the bread and paper early and did a little shopping. Today is a holiday in France as well, so not much was happening in Thenon. Last night the Brières called to invite us to dinner tomorrow night. They both seem well. Pauline retired in February and they would like to go south to the Basque country, but prices are very high there.

We did some gardening and things today and then went over to Sergeac in the afternoon to watch the cycle race and see people. Claude and Mme D. were both well, but looking a bit older. We saw M. Galand, who did our pool surround: he was weaving nicely. I also saw M. Mailly from Marseille, up here for the weekend, with some of his grandchildren it seemed (not the ones I recognised). The race was the same as usual. Six riders quickly broke away from the main pack and the rest broke up into smaller groups. The ones at the end seemed to lose interest fairly quickly and we passed one of them who had given up and gone home. Then back to the house.

The weather forecast for today was not very good, but the day turned out quite well – sunny in the morning and overcast in the afternoon. Fires again tonight, I think. The heating man comes tomorrow. That will be good, as we are all feeling the strain of not being able to bathe or shower.

Tuesday, 22 April 2003

Today the central heating man is supposed to come. It is now 10.30am and Heather and Jenny have gone to market. I am waiting in case he comes this morning, although he is not expected until this afternoon. We have a few things to do today.

The lawn needs mowing again – it rained yesterday and during the night and this has encouraged the grass to grow. We also need to gather some twigs for kindling – we get through it very quickly with two fires going – and have decided to tie it together in bunches to keep it neat and to save storage space.

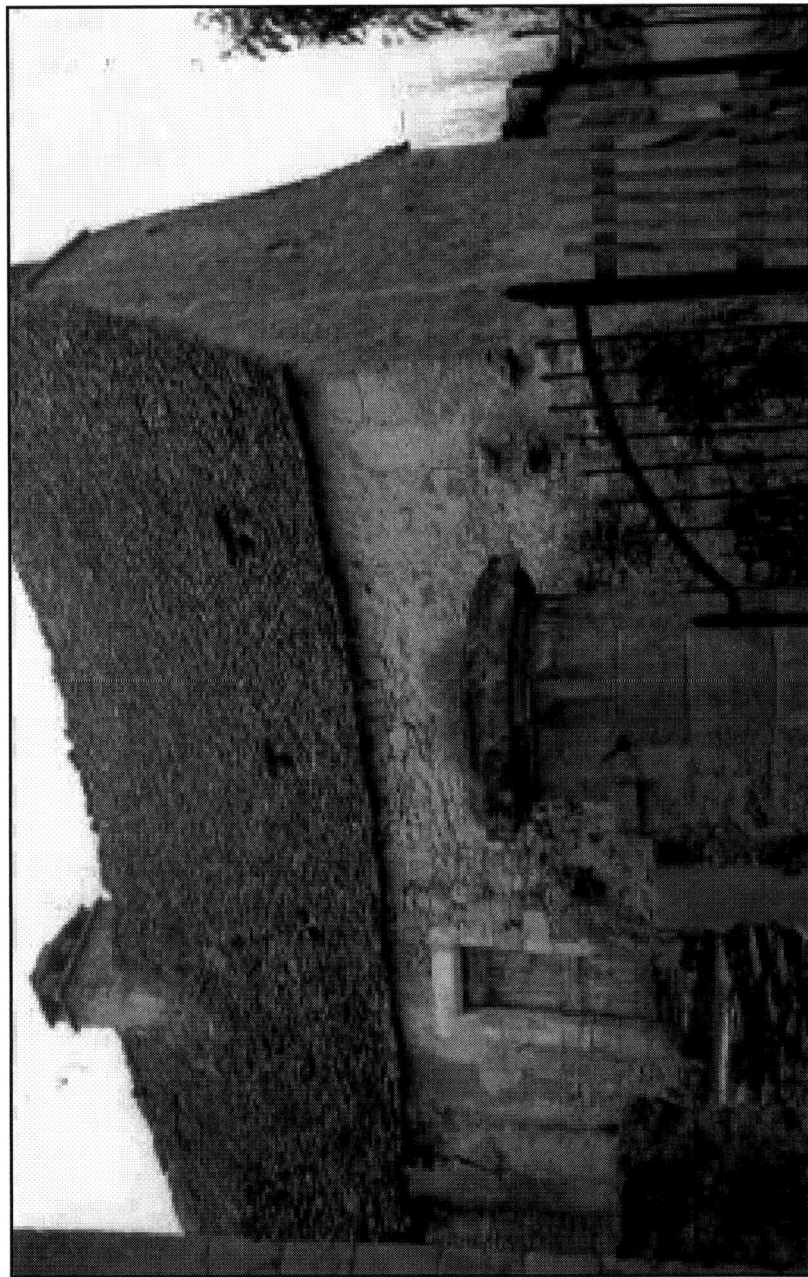

The house at Sergeac in 1972, shortly after we bought it.

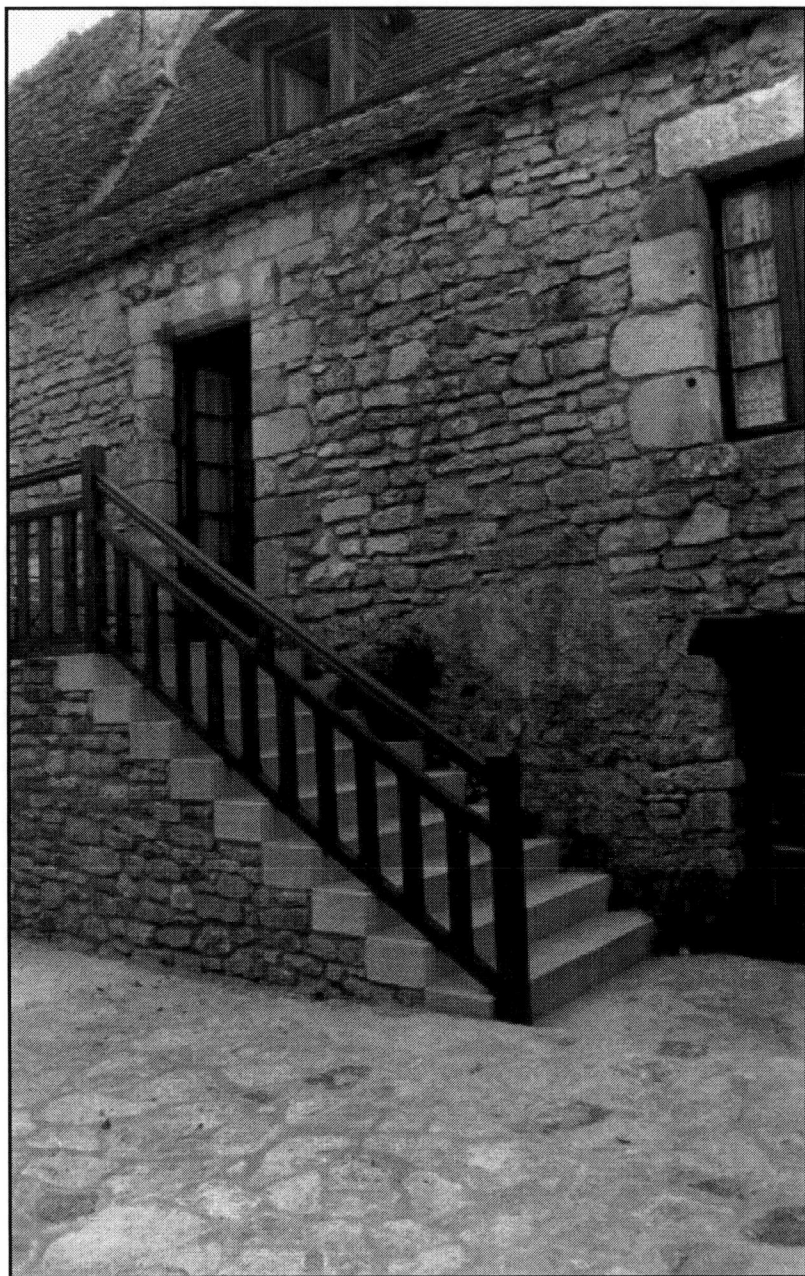

The house at Sergeac in 1990, when we sold it.

The house at Le Jarripigier.

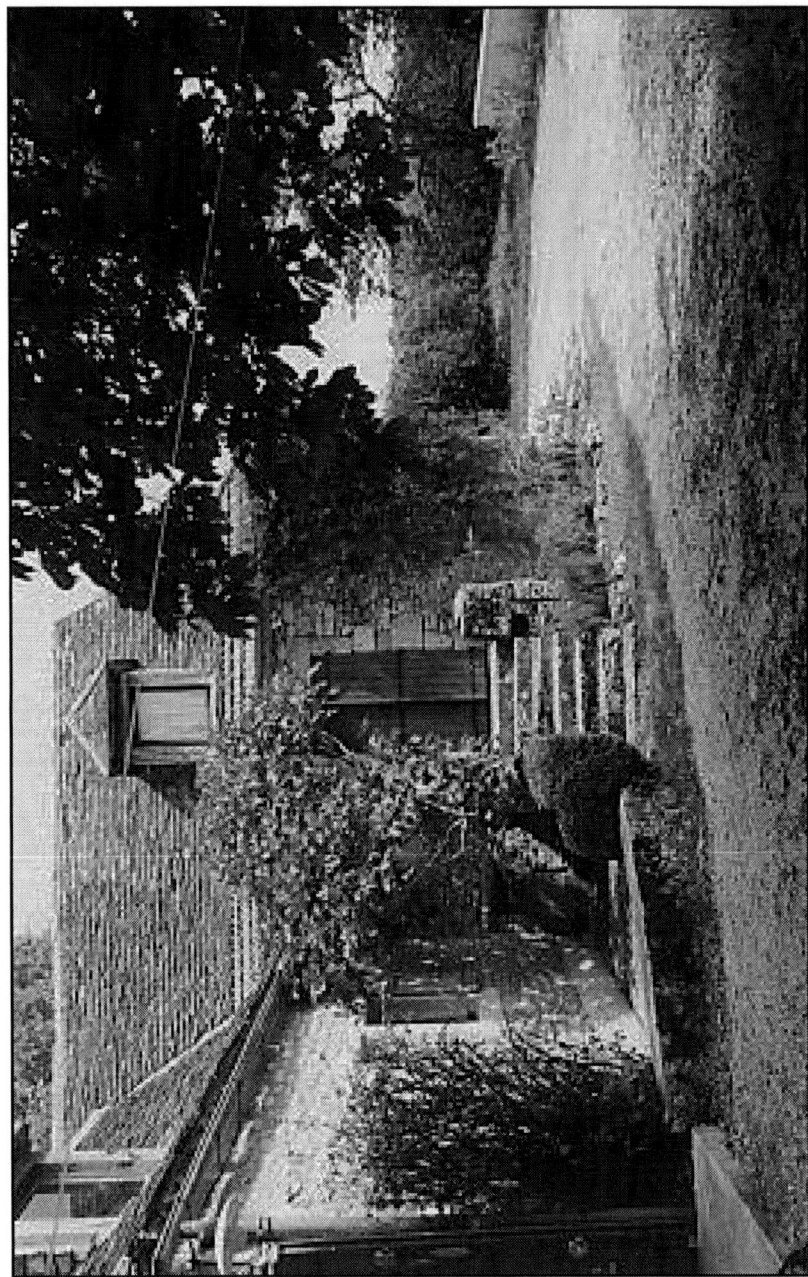

The house at Le Jarripigier, view from the garden.

We have also been looking at the ground by the gas tank. This is the untidiest part of the garden and we think we could plant some ground-cover plants there, such as euonymous. This would cover it and keep it attractive and at the same time require little maintenance. I can't find many ideas in the gardening books I have here, nor on the websites. I shall have to look harder at home. We also need to sort out the lightbulb in our room, which I can't quite reach, cut back some branches that are touching the bathroom window, get some woodworm treatment and possibly some printer ink. So we think we shall go to Perigueux tomorrow.

It is, by the way, a lovely day, although the forecast was not too good.

The man from Depannage Gaz arrived at about 4.45pm. We were getting bit worried by then and I phoned Dominique Aubin's number and they confirmed that we were on the list. The afternoon isn't over yet, the young lady pointed out, and ten minutes later he arrived. The problem was quite simple and more or less what I thought it was. The water pressure was too low to ignite the gas heater. The tap at the back for refilling the water system had been turned so far the wrong way that it had got stuck. So the water pressure just got lower and lower. He told me that all I had to do in future was to pull the blue manette down and then turn to the left (NOT the right) and it refills. He got the water pressure up to just under 2.0 bar and the hot water worked a treat. I had tried turning the old immersion heater on but I think the whole thing was disconnected. Anyway, I turned it back from *force marché* (fast) to *normale* (normal). So tonight (it is now 6.30pm) we had a bath and Jenny will have a shower. What a relief! In a few minutes we are off to the Brières'.

We said goodbye to the Smiths, who are off to Paris in the morning. They took the Dartinsets to the Relais des Chasseurs, where Sylvie is waitressing, and had a very good meal. She was completely taken by surprise. The restaurant was full, mostly with workers from the new autoroute.

The perfect weather has continued right up until now. Sunny and warm and we have hot water as well. A bonus, but the weather is perhaps the chief thing.

Wednesday, 23 April 2003

Another gorgeous day. It is 11.30am and I had to wear sunglasses out
in the garden. We had dinner with the Brières last night. It was very
nice indeed. Pauline had cooked something typically Basque, a meat
casserole with tomatoes and rice, with a lovely lettuce salad. We went
to bed feeling tired but clean, thanks to the man who fixed the water
heater.

Today we went to Rouffignac to get a few things. We bought bread
at the Shopi and some woodworm killer at the hardware shop next
door, plus nails etc. We met Mary there and said we would go round
this evening. She had just taken her daughter to the doctor, but the
queue was so long she had popped out to do the shopping. The main
reason why we went to Rouffignac is that we didn't want to go to
Perigueux. It's too hot. I have to go at some stage to get an air filter
for the Honda. Rain is forecast for the end of the week, so we might
do it then.

We got back and shortly afterwards Anne Trouvé[23] phoned. Her
sons have bought a house at Bars, which they are doing up. She also
has one near Hautefort. I said we are coming down again in July and
we hope we shall see them then, either up here or in Bordeaux.

The Smiths went back this morning. I think I might have heard
their car go past. This morning at about 8.30am Heather saw a deer.
It was in the maize field next door when a tractor started and the
noise apparently scared it, because it ran down the bank and across
our garden, making for the woods and safety.

Thursday, 24 April 2003

Once again the weather is better than forecast. It is cloudy, but there
is still some sun and it is very warm. We got up about 7.30am and had
a shower. Then off to Thenon for bread and the paper. It seems that
the A89 is taking longer than forecast and everyone is blaming
someone else. The autoroute company is blaming delays by
politicians and administrators. The section from Terrasson to
Thenon won't be open until 2006, it seems, and the section from
Thenon to Perigueux will be ready by January next year. That won't
help us very much. Apparently part of the problem is environmental
– some people are insisting on tunnels in some areas, but this adds to
the cost and tunnels are also more dangerous than open roads. As a

result all road tunnels have to have two tubes, not one. This is as a result of the Mont Blanc tunnel fire some years ago.

We were due to go to see Jan and Mary last night, but she phoned to ask us to go tonight. She had to take her daughter to school in Sarlat and it would have been too much of a rush for them. So we shall go tonight instead. Heather and I plan to go to Perigueux this morning and we shall probably have lunch there as well. Jenny wants to stay here. We have to get the air filter for the mower and some ink for the printer. The mower needs a filter quite badly, as it is pumping out black smoke and sometimes doesn't seem very keen on going at all. I shall buy the filter and then let Jan fix it.

It is now 6.10pm. We got the filter and we are going to Jan's tonight, so I shall tell him then. We had lunch at the Lou Chabrol, one we have been to before. A very nice meal for 14.50 euros. I had a salad to start (lettuce, eggs, delicious sauce), then we both had steaks with mushroom sauce and a dessert – Heather had strawberries and I had an ice cream. We wandered around Perigueux, vaguely looking for presents, then came home. Parking was a problem, because the car park we use was half-closed and people had crammed into the other half so tightly that it was impossible to get round. We went down to the river and parked there, free of charge. We bought some wood stain in Rouffignac (M. Bricolage was shut when we got there after lunch) and Jenny used that on the gates, while Heather painted woodworm killer on the cupboards in the kitchen, although this does not seem a very serious problem because we haven't seen any woodworm dust since we arrived and swept it up. We still have to put stuff down for the fouines in the loft. One of them has peed on the trapdoor and we have to clean that up and then put lots of Airwick and other smellies down to deter them. The fact that the house is occupied seems to be the best deterrent, because we heard one the first night, but after we banged on the walls and made a lot of noise it ran off and we have heard nothing ever since.

Friday, 25 April 2003

Once again the weather is better than forecast. It is now 10.55am and the sun is shining and although the *Sud-Ouest* says it will cloud over it isn't doing so as yet. We had breakfast – our last one for this holiday – outside by the pool, listening to the birds and watching the buzzard in the distance.

We went to Jan and Mary's last night and today Heather and I both have slight hangovers. The trouble is that you don't notice you have had too much until the next day. Jenny drove so I didn't have any reason to stop, except of course that I did, as I discovered this morning. I didn't get up until nine and Heather didn't get up until about eight, which is late for both of us. Our main task today is to get some wine to take home. There is not much to do here apart from that. A bit of house cleaning etc., but that won't take long and neither will the packing. We hope to be on our way before eight.

Each day we have been here, more and more plants have bloomed. The ceanothus by the pool looks splendid, with its bright blue flowers. The weigela is now out and the lime tree, which towers over everything, is now covered in leaves. There were hardly any two weeks ago.

Fanny the dog from over the road visits us every day. She thinks our garden is her own private toilet. The hot weather has led to the water in the pool evaporating quite rapidly. It was quite deep on the cover when we arrived, but now the puddle has almost gone. We have gathered up the leaves on the cover and dumped them – one job that M. Courcaud won't have to do. He is coming to open the pool on 12 May.

We have done quite a lot this time, in between relaxing and doing nothing. Meals with the Brières and Smiths were very pleasant, as were drinks with Jan and Mary. Quite a lot of talk about Iraq and general agreement that Bush is not the best thing since sliced bread. But there has been no sign of anti-British feeling, nor anti-American if it comes to that. The French are puzzled by it all and rather fearful about America's economic power. They hope the tourists won't stay away this summer.

Saturday, 3 May 2003

Back home again. We had a fairly easy journey with not too much traffic. It rained at first but after Paris the sun came out and it was glorious weather in England. The traffic was quite bad north of Paris, which is unusual.

A few notes on planting. The ceanothus by the pool is doing well and was in flower while we were there. So was Gertrude Jekyll, which is looking much better now. We cut out the yucca by the cave door. It is too big and has started to take over the whole bed. I planted a euonymus on the bank by the driveway and we have put in some liberated laurels further along, where the old compost heap used to be. We also put in some clematis by trees on the pool side of the wood and in the white alley. One of the clematis that is already there is growing very well and is already far up the tree it is planted against.

Tuesday, 8 July 2003

We arrived early in the afternoon. A fairly leisurely drive down, stopping twice, first at Troyes, where we stayed at the Hotel de la Poste. Rather grand. I booked it from England. Troyes, by the way, is pronounced "Trois". The bill came to 125 euros, which included breakfast and the garage, but not dinner. The restaurant looked good, but very pricey, so we went out and ate at Maitre Kanter, a popular place in the pedestrian street, just a short distance from the hotel. The bill came to 58.90 euros. Troyes seemed like a very lively place. There were lots of people out and the streets seemed busy.

The next night we stayed at the Lion d'Or at Gouzon. I can't say the welcome was all that great. They didn't seem to mind if we stayed or not, but the rooms were clean and ours had a rather nice terrace for sitting out on. It was the sort of French hotel that perhaps existed ages ago. The cupboards and wardrobes were old and solid, ornately carved. The stairways and corridors were dark and twisted and turned. The lights were the sort that you have to push on (finding the switch is difficult in the dark) and then they go out again to save electricity just as you have reached the darkest bit. The meal was fine. We had the 23 euro menu and if anything it was too much. I had bad indigestion as a result.

The next morning we moved on, picking up the motorway at Limoges and getting off just after the Porte de Correze. Glorious sunshine all the way, although the long-range forecast had been for rain.

The house was fine when we arrived. The pool was a bit green, but Mary had warned us about that and had at least left the filter on. The trouble was the bag was clogged and the hot weather meant that the algae had built up. Also we think that maybe there was a lot of ash in the water, because the house over the road has had the roof taken off and it seems that there have been a few bonfires over there. So we changed the bags five times and vacuumed the pool and gradually it got better.

Wednesday, 9 July 2003

Another hot day, although it was cloudy at first. We were both tired yesterday and didn't have much to eat. This morning I still felt quite sleepy, but we went to Leclerc to get some cleaner bags and then had a late breakfast by the pool. The water is looking much cleaner and I don't think the algae is now a problem – just the dirt, which isn't nearly as bad as it was.

However, it seems that the mower is causing problems. Perhaps the oil is too rich, but anyway it shoots out a lot of black smoke and when I tried it yesterday it started okay and then just faded away. Jan says that the blade mount had become detached, so that it was gouging out on one side. He fixed that. But I might have to have it serviced for the other problem. The Husqvarna place on the N89 seems to be open and the mechanic there is good. Maybe he can do it. Whoever does it will have to come and collect it though.

Thursday, 10 July 2003

Another hot day. It must be up near 40 degrees. Quite an exciting day as well. In the first place, we had problems with the pool. It was dirty when we arrived, but we thought we had solved that. Unfortunately last night it started going cloudy and by this morning it was still bad. I put in some anti-algae and hoovered away, changing the bag every fifteen minutes or so, but it was still bad, so I phoned M. Courcaud, who came in the afternoon and said that what we should do is put in some Chlore Choc or Eau de javel. He had a big can of it, and he poured about half into the pool and said that we should change the bag tonight and again tomorrow and by then it should be okay. Apparently this sort of thing happens all the time. So we shall have to wait and see. He said that putting anti-algae in is worse than useless. You should only do that before it goes green: after that it is too late and you will do more harm than good.

Friday, 11 July 2003

Hot again. When we got into the car at 9.30am the temperature was 26 degrees. Later, after the car had been in the sun, it was 35. The pool seems to be clearing up. The filter bags are not clogging up and the nasty scum on the surface has gone. You can see the bottom of the steps and I think that by late afternoon it will be better still. I did add some water because the level was very close to the edge and the pump seems to be labouring a bit.

We bought some more Eau de javel (20 litres) and might put some in if necessary, but I don't think it will be. I telephoned Edward and Alex Roch yesterday. They were just about to phone us and have invited us over for lunch on Monday, so that is something to look forward to. I tried to start the mower this morning but it wouldn't start, so I went to Husqvarna and the mechanic will come on Tuesday at 1.30pm to collect it and generally service it. Jan said the blades need sharpening, so I will get him to do that as well. Having Husqvarna there is very useful, because the mechanic is very good and they are so close that it is easy to get in touch with them. I tried to phone Anne and Michel but got no answer, so I will send them a card.

Saturday, 12 July 2003

Hot again. Yesterday it reached 35 degrees at least and the pool was 27 degrees. The farmers are complaining and the *Sud-Ouest* reported that the maize, strawberry and walnut crops in the southern part of the department are under threat from drought. Yet the water pressure still seems high, so they must have had quite a lot of rain earlier in the year. The pool is still cloudy but getting better. I phoned M. Courcaud yesterday and he said to leave it – do not put in any more Eau de javel or Chlore Choc. Just let it get better slowly, which it is doing. The filter bags are not clogging up as they did before, so really it is just a question of time. We think we might try a swim this afternoon.

The house over the road has lost its roof at last. It seems that it has been removed, perhaps because it was becoming a safety hazard. The tiles have been piled up neatly, so I think that they must be planning to rebuild it, although no one has done any work on it since we have been here. We were told that the lady who bought it wanted to pull it down and put up a new house, but couldn't get permission because the garden was too small. So maybe she is just going to rebuild it. Our house looks much better without the fig tree. H. is very pleased because the replacement fig is growing nicely, but almost the best thing is the wisteria by the pool. This is spreading upwards and outwards and provides a very nice screen. It is also growing over the gate arch, which is beginning to look very pretty. The lawn has not grown very much – just too hot, and the wrong time of year.

Things to do: weed the path, clear up the lime tree leaves, which are everywhere.

Tuesday, 15 July 2003

Yesterday we went over to Altillac to see Edward and Alex Roch. They were both well and we had lunch with them and the artists who are down there at the moment – one group arrived while we were there. We had a most enjoyable time, a light lunch with a perfect flan and salad, followed by cheese and melon. We came back via Turenne, which is absolutely spectacular, a castle perched high on a hill, dominating the valley below. It is about a two-hour drive away. The roads were very quiet, and most of the towns and villages were as well. Not much goods traffic on the roads, since it was the National Day and most of the cars we saw were tourists. We got back here at about 7.15pm and decided to go for a swim. The pool is improving steadily and you can see the bottom quite well now. It is not as dirty as I feared and we shall probably try hoovering tomorrow – I don't want to mess it up now that it is looking respectable.

We knew that Thenon was having a 14 July fireworks display and decided to walk down to the lake, which is where we thought it was going to be. When we got there we found lots of people eating, but no sign of fireworks or other jollifications. So we started to walk back – quite tiring, especially as the heat was quite oppressive. At 11.20pm there was big bang behind us and the display started, but by then we were two-thirds of the way up the hill and only wanted to get home. So we struggled on. We saw flashes from the direction of Auriac and heard lots of bangs from Thenon. But I can't claim that we saw a single firework.

Today is once again sunny, but there was a mist and the chairs and table by the pool were wet. We think this is a sign that there will be rain, with thunder, tomorrow at the latest, as the weather forecasts say.

Wednesday, 16 July 2003

Last night we had a huge storm, with lots of thunder and lightning and rain as well. The forecast is for more of the same. The storm was worst in Bordeaux, according to the *Sud-Ouest*, but it was pretty bad here. The weather during the day was sultry and very hot. We went to Commargue in the afternoon. It is just as impressive as when we first saw it, and you can see Laussel across the valley very well. But you have to park at the top of the road and then walk down 600 metres and, of course, you have to walk back again. Not much fun in the heat of the afternoon. The castle is still ruined, but very impressive. To get in now costs 5 euros a person – the first time we went it was free – but it is still hard work clambering over the ruins. Apparently the castle was simply abandoned because it was so inaccessible and gradually people forgot it was there. It is good to see that it is now being opened to the public again.

We did a little shopping in Rouffignac on the way back and got home some time after 6pm. Heather pointed out a cloud, the first we have seen this holiday, and then more appeared, some of them quite dark. Then we began to hear rumbles of thunder from the direction of Terrasson and we started putting away furniture, pulling out plugs and so on. By nightfall it was still thundering and during the night lightning came as well and it began to rain. Some time after 1am there was a huge clap of thunder that sounded as though it came from the loft. It woke both of us up. By dawn the storm had moved away and the rain eased off. The filter basket in the pool was full of leaves, but apart from that we didn't seem to suffer much damage at all. We couldn't get through on the Internet, because it could not get a dialling tone, but the phone works so it must be something here.

Soon after 9am we had a phone call, from Motoplaisance, about the mower. There is a problem with the mower blades. They do not turn horizontally but a bit out of line. This means that the round disc on which the blades are mounted will have to be replaced. This cannot be done by tomorrow, but it should be alright on Saturday. I might have to phone Jan and see if he can arrange something next week if it is not fixed by Saturday. I would like to give the lawn a trim before we leave, as the rain will no doubt make the grass grow.

We hoovered the pool in the late morning but were still worried because it was taking so long to clear. So I phoned M. Courcaud, who asked what the pH level was. I said it was too low. He said that was impossible and it turned out that it was in fact too high. So we went to Rouffignac and bought some Baisse le pH and put some in, also five Chlore Choc pellets. They seem to have done some good. The pool looks blue, rather than green and the water is definitely not so dirty as it was. But it is still taking an awfully long time to get better.

Still, we have learned a few things:

- If the pool is green do NOT add anti-algae. It is too late. Put in Eau de javel or Chlore Choc.

- Check the pH. If it is too high put in something to lower the pH.

- Change the filter bags regularly, whenever they start to clog up. If it is very dirty when you start hoovering the bags will need changing after fifteen minutes. This is especially true if you have put in anti-algae, since the dead algae cling to whatever dirt is already there.

- Keep the pump on as long as possible.

In the afternoon we decided to go on a tour of the Auvézère, which is supposed to be very pretty. We took our drawing things, but in the end it rained most of the time and so we gave up and came back. We were both tired, so we didn't mind too much.

The *Sud-Ouest* was full of stories about the storm, which it compared with the storm of '99. At the same time, the paper had articles about the drought, which is now affecting most departments in the area.

Thursday, 17 July 2003

We went to the Mule Blanche for dinner last night and actually ordered à la carte rather than a menu. Very bold for us. It was very good. Heather had an enormous salad parisien (ham, cheese, lettuce, etc.) to start with and I had soup. Then we both had magret de canard in a rich sauce, with mashed potatoes and what we thought might be salsify. Then cheese and coffee.

Back at the house the pool is better but still not perfect. This morning (it is now 8.15am) I put in some more Chlore Choc and some Baisse le pH. At least the greenness has gone.

So has the lightbulb in the cave. I changed it but the light still doesn't work. So I'll have to get an electrician to have a look at it. A bulb in the computer room has also gone. I shall do that after breakfast.

The weather is now fine and actually rather chilly, but there has been a heavy dew overnight and there might be some more rain today. We certainly need it, or at least the farmers do.

We saw Pauline Brière yesterday and gave her some chocolates. Roger was working at Ajat. Jerome is in Toulouse and seems reasonably happy there. It is a typical problem for young people here. They have to go away to get work and a future. Maybe that is part of Sylvie's problem.

Friday, 18 July 2003

Bright and sunny, but not so hot as it was before the storm. The pool is looking quite good, although still not perfectly clear. But the water is definitely not blue and the pH level is just right. I put in a little more Chlore Choc.

Yesterday Jan came over and I talked to him about the pool and what needs to be done. Then we had a look at the cave lights. He figured out why the lights don't work (there was a broken bulb in one socket). We took it out and changed to a new bulb and then realised that you have to have both switches on to make the lights work. If the switch inside is turned off, the lights don't work. Anyway, that problem is now solved.

The only one now remaining is the computer. It has not connected to the Internet since the storm and it is possible that the thunder somehow affected it. It was still plugged in when the storm occurred. I have tried the phone upstairs and the extension works, but the PC connection doesn't. I tried the telephone line connected to the PC and that doesn't work and then I tried the PC connection line downstairs with the phone and that doesn't work either. So the line that normally connects the PC to the telephone extension is faulty and it seems as though there is a problem in the PC as well. It looks like a new computer.

The present one is anyway quite out of date – it only has Windows 95 – and the hard disc is practically full. The decision to be made is what sort of PC. I think a portable one would be better. We can take that home with us and even use it at home if we want to. I bought a computer magazine today and we plan to go to Leclerc this afternoon, but I think I will probably get one in Britain and bring it down with me.

We have done a little drawing and painting and are both quite interested in watercolour pencils. They seem to combine the quickness of watercolour with the definition of pastels. We both wish we had done more while here, but unfortunately it was so hot that we couldn't move, let alone paint.

Last night we went to the Peyrol for dinner. We both had the 19 euros menu, the highlight of which was a perfect confit de canard. Jeanine does do the best confits in the district. We had a bottle of Pecharmant with it. We ate outside and it was superb. Jeanine came to say hello, but her daughter served us. She looks much like her mother.

Saturday, 19 July 2003

Our last day. We ate in last night – a Spanish omelette, to get rid of some of the things we have got left over. Tonight we shall go out. I went to Husqvarna and the man there said the mower would be delivered at 1.30pm, which means I shall have some mowing to do this afternoon. Although the grass hasn't grown very much, some of the weeds have and it is beginning to look untidy. I washed the car, as always missing one or two bits – the car wash is much better. Another hot day, but not so hot as before the storm. The pool was 26 degrees this morning and looks much cleaner and bluer. I gave it a vacuum and shall do it again later. We plan to aim for the Loire tomorrow and then move on to Normandy or somewhere like that the next day and then get a ferry around late morning. We have to go to the ferry office because the girl at Dover didn't give us our return ticket, just the ticket out.

Tuesday, 22 July 2003

Back home. On Sunday we had a trouble-free drive to Chartres, where we stayed at the Grand Monarque Hotel. Close to the town centre and apparently the best in town, but it was very expensive and not all that wonderful. The room cost 102 euros and breakfast was 11 euros a head. The restaurant was closed (it was a Sunday) and so we went to the brasserie where the food was okay, but two dinners cost 40.30 euros. We walked around Chartres a little but Heather's foot was blistered and hurting so we went back to the hotel.

The next day we set off to go to Dieppe, but in the event the traffic was so light and travelling so easy that we went on to Calais and caught a ferry at 2pm. From Dover to home the traffic was heavier than we had seen it all the time we were in France.

On Saturday, I went to Husqvarna and the mower was ready. It was delivered just after lunch. It works much better now, with no nasty black smoke coming out. The main problem was with the blades. They needed sharpening, but the disc on which they are mounted had to be replaced. That cost 113 euros, and replacing the blades another 30.60. The total bill came to 301.70 euros, which I thought was quite reasonable, since it hadn't been serviced ever since I bought it.

Saturday, 6 September 2003

We arrived yesterday by train. As usual, we caught the 9.23am Eurostar from Ashford arriving in Paris two hours later. Then we crossed Paris by taxi to Austerlitz and had lunch in the buffet. I had a salad, which was quite good, but Heather didn't think much of her croque monsieur. The train left Paris at 14.02 and got to Brive at 17.58, after stopping at Limoges and Uzerche. It was quite comfortable – a trolley with food and drinks came round and we had some water – but the seats were quite small and we were both tired and stiff when we got off. The car was a Citroën hired from Citer in the Rue Edouard Herriot. It was raining when we left and this gradually turned into a thunderstorm. There were traffic jams at Larche, caused by the traffic lights, but by the time we got to Le Jarripigier the storm had passed. We dumped our stuff and then went into Montignac for a meal at the restaurant by the river – the Lascaux I think it's called. A very nice meal. Heather began with smoked salmon while I had melon in Monbazillac – very good, easy and an idea for home. I had confit for the main course and Heather had a steak. We got there at about 8.30pm. There were not many people there and Montignac itself seemed deserted. A very definite end of season, autumnal feeling about everything.

We went to bed tired and both slept well. This morning we had a look around and discovered that there have been quite a few changes, even in a few weeks since our last visit.

First, the pool is looking cleaner than it has all year. Jan and Mary have been looking after it and it seems that the secret lies in the element or electrode – the bit that is rather like the element in a kettle. A friend of theirs had a look at it and discovered that it was completely furred up, not surprising in this area of hard water. They took it and cleaned it up with some special acid that dissolves limescale. They then put it back and since then the pool has been much cleaner. I have to go to Desjoyaux to prepare the hivernage and I shall tell them about this. It should have been done. It seems as though the limescale has been building up for years and preventing the element from working properly.

Second, the house over the road is being rebuilt. The roof was taken off early in the summer and now there is scaffolding all over and the garden has been cleared. Apparently the people who bought it are going to restore it and then sell it.

Third, this morning we watched the people in the field next door harvesting the maize. It was very impressive. A big harvester drove round the crop (six hectares in size, according to Jean-Paul), with a team of three lorries following it. The harvester cut the maize, strimmed off the ears of corn and then shredded the rest of the plants, pouring a continuous stream of silage into the waiting lorries.

It was very misty early in the morning, but this cleared and although it wasn't very sunny it was quite warm. A few spots of rain, but nothing much. We went to Rouffignac to buy some cement – the corner of the pool needs fixing, as does the door to the tractor shed. I also bought some Round Up to spray on the drive. But the forecast is not good. Lots of rain for the next few days.

Sunday, 7 September 2003

Jan and Mary came over this morning. I owed them 50 euros, which didn't seem very much. They explained about the pool. Part of the reason why it was not clear was because the electrode or element, which is in the mechanism, was furred up. This fits into a pipe under the white plastic cover. Over a period of time limescale had built up until the element could not be seen. Jan showed me how to take it out and we discovered that it was once again becoming encrusted. We took it out, after turning the motor and electricity off, and tomorrow I shall take it to Desjoyaux. Why is it getting encrusted? And how often has it been cleaned? To get the limescale off you have to soak it in acid, which you can buy in any DIY shop. I shall get some tomorrow and then I shall phone Jan and get him to help me put it back again.

They have some Dutch friends who are looking for a house in the area. We wondered if the time had come to think about selling the house. It is beginning to become something of a headache at times. Mary will speak to them to see if they are interested. But we don't know what the house is worth. About 200,000 euros, I reckon. We shall see.

The weather is lousy. It is cold and raining. Quite a change from a week ago. Apparently it will stay like this for the rest of the week. Lucky us.

Monday, 8 September 2003

Another wet, dreary day, just as forecast. But quite an eventful one as well. We told Jan and Mary that we were planning to sell and they said they had some Dutch friends who were looking for a bigger house in the area – at the moment they live not far from Plazac. They came over this morning at 11am and we showed them around. They were very pleasant and seemed to like the place – he is an actor, and they spend most summers here. They want a house they can move straight into. Of course, we were not really ready. We don't have any idea about prices and the house wasn't really ready. We want to give it some paint before we sell it and the cracks in the kitchen look quite bad, although they have not really got much worse. Anyway, in the afternoon we went off to Terrasson to arrange for the hivernage. I took the pool electrode and they, or rather the woman there, agreed that it was not very good that it should go like that so quickly. It should be cleaned during the hivernage, she said. She didn't really believe that it had probably never been cleaned. She phoned M. Courcaud on his mobile to see if he could do the hivernage this week, but she had to leave a message. I bought some acid in Weldom while we were there and put it in a plastic bottle, diluted with four parts water to one of acid, and then put the electrode in that. It fizzed and bubbled away and started dissolving the limescale immediately. If M. Courcaud comes this week I shall ask him about the limescale. It shouldn't happen. That explains why the pool was so bad this year, and probably last year as well.

We wanted to get a valuation on the house, but the Wilson's agency at the top of the town and the one at the bottom were both closed, as were most shops because it is Monday. So we shall have to do that tomorrow, when we go to the market.

Tonight we plan to eat in Perigueux.

Wednesday, 10 September 2003

We did eat in Perigueux, at Lou Chabrol, a place we have been to before. We both had confit, which I thought was not the best I have ever had – the skin was not crispy enough. But the potatoes, done in a round and sprinkled with nutmeg, were lovely as was the little omelette, also done in a round.

Today was quite pleasant, from the weather point of view. Cloudy but sunny as well and it did not rain until evening. I got up and put the electrode back in the pool machine. It was quite easy and seems to have worked, but the motor seems to be running hot – maybe it always does that, but I have never noticed it before.

Then we went in to Sarlat where I arranged for Heather to be able to access my bank account – easier than changing it to a joint account. Then we came back and waited for someone from the estate agents Wilson's to come around. It turned out to be a lady named Gil, who is based in Le Bugue. She did a tour and said it was a medium property, worth somewhere around £140,000, which is more or less what I expected. She said we might have to pay some capital gains tax, but this goes down according to the number of years you have owned it and you can also claim for improvements made, such as the pool, central heating and so on. I shall have to dig out all the bills when I get home. Heather has not been well today – it might have been something to do with the rich food we have been eating. Tonight we eat in. We lunched in Sarlat. Not wonderful.

Thursday, 11 September 2003

Today M. Courcaud and his partner arrived to do the hivernage. I told him about the electrical problem and he looked at it and said that the heating was caused by the Sterilor unit. I think this might have to be replaced, but that can be done next spring when the *mise en service* takes place. They put the cover on and put some special hivernage liquid in and the whole thing did not take long at all. M. C. said that the water here is so hard that you quite often have to clean the electrode twice a season, because the limescale builds up. This could also explain why the water pressure seems low, especially when it comes to filling the bath etc. with hot water.

Heather was feeling better today – it might just have been something she ate. After M. Courcaud had gone I mixed up some concrete and put it on the entrance to the mower shed – that should make it easier to get in and out. At present the ramp is quite steep. I put away the wheelbarrow, hosepipe and other tools and really we had done more or less everything by 4pm. Our Dutch friend rang to say that they don't want the house – just after I rang them an estate agent phoned to say that an offer they made on another house has been accepted. This is not really a blow as we were not expecting to sell that easily. We shall get things ready and collect some photos and then let Wilson's have it when we come down in the autumn.

We drove around a little this morning – possible last looks etc. We both feel a little sad at the idea of not coming here again or at least not coming to our house and Heather says she will miss the garden most of all. But the journey and all the hassle will begin to get too much and anyway, we want to go to other places.

Today is supposed to be cold and rainy, but instead it is warm and sunny. The grass is beginning to grow, thanks to all the rain. There is evidence that there have been some storms here; we saw quite a few uprooted walnut trees. Generally speaking, everything now seems to be settling down for the autumn. It has not been a great season for tourism, with hotel bookings down and restaurants not doing too well. Maybe the weather elsewhere was so good that people did not feel the need to come to France and, of course, the Americans seem to have stayed at home this year. There was quite a lot in the *Sud-Ouest* this morning about the anniversary of 9/11, which the Americans are determined not to forget.

Sunday, 26 October 2003

We came down yesterday, by car with Jenny. It was a lovely sunny day, but very cold and it was still cold this morning. M. Barbini's field was covered in frost, but there was no frost where the trees provided shelter and the temperature on the car was only -1 degree. Still, it is a lot colder than it has been for this year. When we arrived we put on the central heating and it has been on ever since. The house has become quite warm but we shall leave the heating on because it takes a long time to heat up the house after it has been empty for so long. Last night we ate at the Hotel de la Grotte in Montignac. Still run by eccentric ladies but the meal was fine. We got back at about 9.30pm and went to bed fairly early.

This morning we went into Thenon and brought bread and a paper and then went to Rouffignac for the market and to buy food for today's meal. The market was quite small but quite lively and there were lots of people there. The quality of the food seemed much better than in the supermarket, something we should have thought about before we did our shopping. The house is warm now, but not baking hot, and the hot water is not really hot – something we noticed in the summer. We have not tried the downstairs shower yet. There seems to be plenty of pressure and the water heater starts as it should, but the water doesn't get very hot.

Monday, 27 October 2003

Another lovely day and not so cold as yesterday. Also, the house has heated up considerably and Heather actually lowered the temperature on the thermostat. We have kept the heating on all the time since we arrived and I reckon at this time of year it takes about two days to heat the brickwork of the house, as well as the air. This morning we took advantage of the sunshine to go out and collect pine cones. They are very good for getting the fire started. But this time we didn't find them so easily as last year. Maybe this is because of the warm summer – perhaps the pines don't produce so many cones if the weather is dry.

We had the kitchen fire on until about 10.30pm last night, by which time it was right down to the last embers. It burns a lot of wood; hence the huge wood piles outside people's houses. I telephoned M. Lascoumes about the water heating and left a message for him to call us. Now that the house is warm the fact that the water isn't very warm doesn't matter too much – we can always boil a kettle for extra heat. But we need to get it fixed.

It is a perfect autumn day. I got the mower out this morning, but the grass was still a bit too wet to do anything. So I sprayed the drive with Round Up and the sprayer got jammed, so I fixed that. Jenny went for a walk and Heather did some sketching. I shall take some pictures and do some sketching myself later. The farmers around are all getting ready for winter. There are bonfires here and there and wood smoke coming from the chimneys. The shops are full of plastic flowers and chrysanthemums, because it is Toussaint next weekend.

Tuesday, 28 October 2003

This morning we went to Thenon market and then went to Le Bugue to give the house keys to the Wilson's estate agency. They are going to put the house on the market at 215,000 euros – about £140,000. This is rather more than we were expecting. Gil, the lady who came to see our house when we were down last month, suggested not mentioning furniture. We could use that as a carrot if someone shows interest. It also means we could perhaps get a little more if we sold and anyway, she says that there is not much of a market for second-hand furniture. I rang Dominique Aubin about the water and someone will come on Friday morning. M. Lascoumes did not phone back last night and anyway the Aubin firm seem very efficient.

Today we had a mystery phone call. The woman on the other end said "Allo" and when I answered she hung up. Trying to sell me double glazing I expect, but more probably she was expecting a woman to answer.

It is warmer today, but cloudy and dull and it actually rained a little this afternoon. We had an omelette for lunch (chopped sage goes well with eggs) and are going out this evening, but we don't know where yet. We saw the Brières this morning and they both seem very well. We have to tell the Dartinsets we are selling.

Thursday, 30 October 2003

Today is overcast and raining, much like yesterday, when we decided to go to Leclerc simply because it was too miserable to do much else. The shop is enormous and there weren't many people there. I quite enjoyed wandering around, looking at things, most of which are so different from what we find at home. We came back, had lunch and in the afternoon Heather and I practised our painting, using a bowl of fruit as a model.

We had a minor worry this morning. When I got up I found we had no water. I phoned the Compagnie des Eaux and the man asked if the neighbours were having problems. Obviously I was the first person he had spoken to. We went to the Smiths, because they have an outside tap, but when we got there we found some English people there. We think they might be the Smiths' daughter and her husband. The lady said yes, they did have water, but it had gone off briefly. So we went home and found the water was working again. We went out to get bread and a paper and on the way back saw a water board van parked by the road near the bottom of the hill, so presumably someone else had reported a problem. When we got back I had a quick shower and shave and there was plenty of water, but it was only warm, not hot. Fortunately, the man is coming tomorrow morning.

Last night we had a nice dinner, with roast veal and roast vegetables. I made a sort of cauliflower gratin – cauliflower, a carrot and some onions boiled and mixed and then put in the oven with breadcrumbs on top. It would be better grilled and perhaps with cheese, nutmeg or something else to add a bit of taste. But well worth working on.

What we shall do today I don't know. It is not very pleasant for the garden and there is not much to do in the house. But we shall find something.

In the end Heather and I went out for a drive in the afternoon. We went to St Cyprien and came back via Le Bugue, but it wasn't very pleasant. It rained most of the time. When we got back Jenny had lit the fire in the kitchen and we spent the rest of the day there, reading and eating.

Friday, 31 October 2003

Halloween. It is becoming quite big in France, as in Britain, encouraged by businesses that have things to sell. But Toussaints remains the main event at this time of the year. The paper says today that there will be special bus services to the main cemeteries in Perigueux and the flower shops have been doing big business selling chrysanths and plastic flowers. It is now 9.50am and we are waiting for the man from Dominique Aubin to arrive. The other day we found a bit of a car – the back spoiler or something lying in the driveway, as if someone had been in to see us and something had fallen off. But we don't know who.

The swimming pool is very full of water and if the rain continues it will soon be overflowing.

We have invited Jan and his family over this evening for an aperitif. It will be nice to see them. I also have to pay Jan 80 euros for work they have done here.

Down at the lake some of the trees by the restaurant have been cut down and they are obviously planning to do something there. It looks a mess at the moment but by next summer will no doubt be much better. Meanwhile, the A89 continues to make progress. The only part that is not more or less finished is the part between Brive and Thenon – the part that most interests us.

Saturday, 1 November 2003

Our last day. Last evening Jan and Mary came over for an aperitif. I paid Jan 80 euros for work done on the garden. I also told him about the water problem. The man from Aubin came yesterday and checked the heater – there was no problem there, he said, so it must be elsewhere in the system. He said that when he turned the hot tap on cold water still came out, which meant that the cold water was not being sealed off properly. The water was lukewarm because cold water was mixing with hot. So I paid 42 euros for very little. Jan said that he knew someone who was a plumber as well as a *chauffagiste* and he will get him to look at it while we are away. It might be a blockage somewhere, but whatever it is, the man will be able to fix it. We also arranged for Mary to come in and look at the house during the winter – it might get cold, as it did earlier this week, in which case it will be useful to have someone keeping an eye on the house, as she did last year.

Yesterday afternoon we went out for a walk, along the road towards Thenon, then down the path to the Norton's old house and on to Vaujean. We turned left down to the road and then right to the path leading back to Vaujean and then left up the hill to the main road. We saw a few people on the way, all of whom seemed friendly and said bonjour.

Today I put up some wire over the cave door for the wisteria to grow along. It grew a lot this year and by next year should be well established on the gable wall. The wisteria over the gate to the pool is also doing very well and will make a very pretty entrance soon.

We went over to see the Dartinsets and told them we were going to sell. They seemed a bit upset.

*   *   *

Friday, 9 April 2004

We arrived last night at 7.15pm and, after dumping the cases and making the beds, we went to the Orée du Bois for dinner. Very nice. Jenny and I had salmon salad to start with and I had faux filet for the main course. The journey down was quite easy, but there were lots of showers on the way. The main excitement was provided by having a flat front tyre, which we discovered as we were about to get off the ferry. It had a bit of air in it, so we went off to Calais and found a supermarket car park (Champion) where we tried to change the wheel but couldn't get the old one off. So I asked someone if there was a tyre shop nearby and he said yes, about 400 metres down the road on the left, Pneu Fauchille. We drove down and they had a new tyre which they put on because the old one was completely bald. It was very lucky finding the place so easily and we only lost about an hour of time. The whole thing cost 163.10 euros.

Today we got the house clean. It wasn't very dirty. The main thing was that Jan's plumber friend had fixed the water. So we now have hot water from all taps and it is better than ever, because the pressure was very low, but the heat still worked. It makes such a difference. The repair cost 40 euros. I shall go to Rouffignac to get the money and will pay Jan today. The cashpoint in Thenon is not working.

I saw the Dartinset family picking leeks from the garden – they clean them and then put them in bags and in the freezer and use them during the year. M. Dartinset showed me the back of the house that was falling down for years. It is in the process of being re-roofed, but the back wall has a huge crack in it, so big that you can see through it. He confidently told me that it would fall down.

Between the Smiths and us someone is building a house and another one is being built on the right-hand side along the road to Thenon. So Thenon is growing. Mme Dartinset said that there are now many English in Rouffignac. She didn't know why.

The Smiths are here as well, but were out when I went to see them. We shall no doubt catch up with them later.

Saturday, 10 April 2004

While we were having breakfast this morning a man knocked on the door and asked the way to M. Smith's house. He was a plumber, going to sort out a problem. Later, Shirley came round to see if I could go along and help translate. This is not always very easy when there is a technical matter to be discussed. In this case it was all fairly simple. I asked the plumber to come round and look at a small leak we have in the upstairs loo, but he had another job to do so he didn't come. I went back home and got the mower working and did some grass cutting. But it is not working very smoothly – I think it needs the spark plug cleaning and possibly some oil. So I put it away with only a little bit of the lawn cut. Heather and Jenny did some pruning and I then sprayed Round Up on the drive. The weeds are under control there, perhaps because of the spraying I did last year. I shall give it a few more goes this time.

Last night we had a beef casserole. I didn't like it very much. The beef was too tough. It should have been cooked for much longer, I think.

Today it is cold and overcast, although the sun is trying to shine. Even so, we have been quite lucky with the weather so far.

Douglas came round this afternoon to have a look at the leaking loo tap. It was not really serious – the tap is too small for a washer. Instead, very fine twine or string is wrapped round the unit, with Vaseline, and tightened. This effectively stops water seeping out. But the tap should not be turned off as often as we do it. In fact, there is no real need to turn off any taps as long as the water is turned off at the main. We have arranged to have lunch with them on Wednesday, the day before they leave.

A young couple has been working on the house over the road. Apparently he is a chef and his idea is to restore the house and then sell it.

Wilson's, the estate agents, are coming round on Thursday morning to talk about selling the house. Now we are again torn. But I think our heads will rule our hearts this time. We cannot keep the house for ever and even the Smiths are talking of selling theirs one day. Although not for some time.

Sunday, 11 April 2004

The Wilsons are bringing some people to see the house on Thursday. I thought at first it was just them. So things are beginning to happen quite quickly.

It is now 11am. Cloudy and dull, but not so cold as it has been. We are going to the Croquant at Fanlac for lunch. We had three 18 euro menus, a bottle of Pecharmant and coffee and the bill came to 71.80 euros. Heather and I had confit and Jenny had gigot. Excellent quality, with lovely potatoes. Cheese and crêpes for dessert. The restaurant was much the same as usual. The patron, Roger Alain, was in charge and looked very smart in his red shirt. There was a Franco-German party in there, who seemed to be related, and various other couples and families. Two children, a boy and a girl, ran around without upsetting anyone except themselves occasionally.

We went round to see Jan and Mary on Friday. They were busy working on the barn, which they are going to convert into a gite. Their daughters Ella and Sally were there as well. It seems that the water problem was actually quite simple. The old hot water boiler was still connected and when we put the hot water tap on water came from there as well but it wasn't hot. I don't think I could have fixed it. But the friend of Jan's who did turned out to be the plumber who installed the tank years ago so he was familiar with the system. All he had to do was turn the hot water heater off and the problem was solved. But I don't understand why it worked before and only started going wrong last year. Anyway, the whole thing works much better now. The hot water is really hot and comes on even when the pressure is low, as it usually is in the upstairs washbasin.

A fairly lazy day yesterday, but we all slept well. Heather says I snored all night even though she kept hitting me. In the end she got fed up and went to sleep herself.

I got the mower working yesterday, but it cut out a few times, maybe because the grass was still wet. I think the spark plug needs to be cleaned, but the machine came without an engine manual and I'm not sure how to get the cover off. Jan said he will come round some time and have a look. I need to cut the lawn before Thursday. Everything else is looking quite good. We saw M. Barbini yesterday. He had lit a fire in the field behind our house and wanted to tell us that. He is a very nice man, small and grizzled. Two years ago he told us to help ourselves to the apples from the tree near our wood, which he said was a pomme des pommiers. They were good, too.

Monday, 12 April 2004

Easter Monday. A very pleasant day, too. Bright and sunny and warmer than yesterday, but still with a rather chilly northern wind. We spent the day working in the garden. I got the mower working and did a bit more, but it is still not perfect and had a tendency to cut out when I put the blades down. I also got the big strimmer working and used two tanks of fuel, but then I couldn't start it again. Heather got the little one going but then the strimming cord ran out and we couldn't take the top off – we couldn't find the wrench that we needed.

Still, the garden looks much better now and H. and I have stopped for the day, while Jenny has gone for a long walk. Such energy.

I am looking out of the window and it is beginning to cloud over. That might be quite good as it should mean that we won't get a frost tonight.

Wednesday, 14 April 2004

Yesterday Jan came over and we looked at the mower. We took the cover off (quite easy if you have the right tools) and then took out the spark plug. It was black with soot. We cleaned it and replaced it and then tried the mower. It started okay and went up and down but didn't really sound very much better. Jan said that he thought there was a problem with the air supply. So we took the air filter off and the mower worked much better. But you can't run the mower for long without the air filter on so that is not a permanent solution. The fact is that it should have been serviced better last year. It was only taken in on 15 July and has not been used very much since then.

I took the two strimmers in to Husqvarna earlier and the mechanic there said that the problem with the big one is that it had the wrong fuel in – two stroke fuel instead of the special strimmer fuel. The smaller one worked, but the head containing the cord was jammed so that we could not get the cord out. The mechanic couldn't free it so I left it with them. But I have to go back today to tell them about the mower. They will have to take it back in.

We went to the market yesterday. It was small and empty-looking. In a few years' time there won't be a market here. The stall that sold footwear has gone and so has the fish stall. Many of the other familiar sights have disappeared as well. But if customers don't go to the market why bother to set up a stall? The market at Le Bugue last year was quite prosperous still.

There are now four estate agents in Thenon. Gil of Wilson's said that they are all trying to extend into the area, because the other ones are pretty well saturated. When the new motorway extension to Brive is open (in 2006) the area should be more popular still.

It is now 9.46am. The sun is coming through and it should be a warm, dry day, just like yesterday. The weather forecast in the *Sud-Ouest* last weekend was not very good for the area, but Mary said that the TV forecast was much better.

Yesterday we had a visit from two English walkers who were part-owners of the house down the hill. They had come down with Peter Hayward and his wife, but they had gone home the previous day. Peter Hayward used to attend meetings at the International Maritime Organization (IMO) and I met him a few times – small world. I didn't get the names of our visitors but their daughter and some friends had stayed at our house some years ago because the house down the hill was double booked. Sue Norton phoned Heather, who said they could use our house, although we were going to be there ourselves. They were all very nice young people and I can't say that I remembered them being there. Anyway, they were very grateful and told their parents that our house was a palace. The Nortons are still co-owners apparently but Mike is not with the Foreign Office any more – he has been lecturing at Tokyo University. They seem to be enjoying themselves in Japan.

We walked around the garden this morning and felt twinges of regret at the thought of selling and not being able to come here again. It was so pretty, now that the lawn has been cut and strimmed and we have put some plants (from the market) in the cistern cover by the driveway.

I went into Thenon today for the paper and got some money out of the bank. Then I went to Husqvarna and told the man about the mower. He was the one who did it last year – I think he is the boss. He said he will come tomorrow (Thursday) afternoon. That makes me feel better. Something is being done.

Roger Brière is around, but the studio was dark and the inner door was locked. He must be out on a site somewhere.

Today we had lunch with the Smiths – they are leaving tomorrow. We went to the Périgord on the Place Tourny in Montignac. A very good meal, which we all enjoyed, including two bottles of Tiregand.

The restaurant is not very picturesque, but it has a lovely view over the river and the service and food are very good. There are more signs of prosperity in Thenon. Down by the lake the house on the left, which has a lovely position, is being restored and enlarged. Apparently it is owned by the manager of the Shopi. The house just round the corner from that, as you go up the hill to Thenon, now has a roof on. It is said to be owned by an Englishman. The centre of gravity in the town seems to be moving up the hill. The old Huit à 8 is still empty and the hardware store has shut down and although the other shops are open, they are not thriving. I think the Shopi has made a difference.

Friday, 16 April 2004

The man from Husqvarna came yesterday and said the air filter was completely dirty and a new one was needed. I said I would go to Perigueux to get one. He suggested that I get a new spark plug, as the old one would certainly need to be replaced as well – cleaning was not enough. So Heather and I set off and got the parts. But although I know how to take the cover off and do the work I don't have the tools needed. So we stopped at Husqvarna and the man said he would come on Tuesday. It was a lovely sunny day and there were signs of spring everywhere. Men were out with their mowers and strimmers and the trees are coming into leaf. We went past the new motorway section which runs from the Mule Blanche to Bordeaux: unfortunately the section we need won't be ready until 2006.

At 11am Gil arrived alone to say the potential buyers (from northern France) had cancelled at the last minute, much to her annoyance because she had come all the way from Le Bugue to Thenon to see them. This happens quite a lot. Heather was annoyed but it had the good effect of making her feel that selling was a good idea after all. Neither of us wants the hassle any more. We spent a lot of the morning cleaning up the house and garden and making it look presentable, so I think it was good for us in other ways. Mary phoned to see how the sale had gone. I told her and she then asked us over to their house for drinks on Saturday evening.

Today we worked in the garden. I did a bit of strimming and Heather and Jenny cleared the bank by the entrance to the driveway. It was covered in brambles and nettles. We came across the inspection cover for the septic tank, something I had forgotten about. By the afternoon Heather and I were tired out, but I expect Jenny will go for a walk.

Saturday, 17 April 2004

A dull miserable day, raining quite heavily this morning. Gil phoned up to say that someone wants to see the house this afternoon: I don't hold out much hope for the people who came yesterday. They were the French people from the north who should have come on Friday but had to cancel. Still, two people in two days is not too bad. At least the house is clean. We have decided to go the Hotel de la Grotte for lunch tomorrow.

Last night we lit the fire in the living room. It really does blaze away and warms the room up a treat. But it gets so warm the thermostat cuts out and the rest of the house feels cold. But today, despite the damp weather, it is not too cold. Just miserable.

At about 11am Heather and I went for a drive. Jenny stayed behind because she was preparing lunch and dinner. We first went to the Shopi petrol station because they have an air pump and one of the back tyres was down. Then we went on to Montignac, past Sergeac, through St Leon and up to the Côte du Jour and then home.

Everywhere looked damp, but spring is here. Some of the trees are green and the cherry trees in the woods added a dash of white that was cheering. The fields are so small in this area, just patches of earth 100 yards long by 50 wide or even smaller. All were neatly ploughed and no doubt ready for sowing. According to the *Sud-Ouest* today the first local strawberries have arrived at the market in Vergt. But they are two weeks late.

Sunday, 18 April 2004

Wet and rainy, cold and overcast. Not a very encouraging day. We are going to Montignac, the Hotel de la Grotte for lunch. Last night we went to Jan and Mary's for drinks. Very pleasant. They are working hard on their gite, which will help to give them an income in later years. We were planning to go out to collect pine cones today, but the weather is too unpleasant. They are excellent fire lighters and help fires to blaze up immediately. We are also going to light the fire in the living room when we get back. It is much more comfortable than the kitchen, although the fire there is more visually appealing. The fact is that the one in the living room works better and the seats are more comfortable. It's a pity we didn't have the thermostat put in the kitchen, because when the heat in the living room reaches a decent temperature, the heating in the rest of the house goes off. This doesn't matter in the summer but at this time of year it does.

We had two people to see the house yesterday – an English couple called Smith. They seemed more promising than the French the day before, but we shall see.

Monday, 19 April 2004

Yesterday we went to the Hotel de la Grotte for lunch. It was actually very good. A taster to start with, green asparagus with a cream sauce, followed by a gesiers salad and then Heather and I both had Piccata de Boeuf followed by dessert. A bottle of Pecharmant and the total bill for three was 100 euros.

Apart from the food, the charm of the place is its eccentricity. The decor is rather Christmassy. Lots of gold drapes over the fireplace and fading artificial flowers. The lady in charge is still there. Charming but rather quaintly dressed, looking old fashioned in a way.

The weather was lousy and it continued like that today. In the morning Heather and I went to Sarlat. We were both feeling a bit hemmed in by the weather, because you can't do much when it is raining all the time. We parked near the town centre and although most shops are closed on Mondays, the tourist ones were open. We sheltered from the rain by having a coffee on the square in the middle of town and watched bedraggled groups of tourists walk disconsolately from arcade to arcade. A family of four sat outside the café, obviously determined to enjoy their holiday, even at the risk of their health. We came home and had some rillettes for lunch, which we bought in Sarlat. The aim was to take it home as presents. I didn't like it – too runny and Heather didn't have any at all. Jenny finished up some soup she had made on Saturday.

In the afternoon Heather and I went out, to get some pine cones for the fire and to do some painting. We went to Belcayre and sat in the car for forty minutes or so, but the rain started again and as we had both done something we decided to come home. We went via Rouffignac and stopped at the Shopi to get a few items of food, including a tin of pâté. We got back just as Jan was arriving to look at the mower. We changed the air filter and plug, but although it start it still didn't sound very good. The man from Motoplaisance is coming tomorrow so I shall tell him about it. Jan thinks it is probably something fairly simple, but it is definitely not the filter.

I shall have to go there in the morning, because we are due to go to Anne and Michel's at Sarrazac for lunch, so I probably won't be here if he comes then.

Tuesday, 20 April 2004

Dull and rainy. The forecast is for brighter spells this afternoon. I went to get the bread and paper and called in at Husqvarna to tell them about the mower. It must be something more serious, said the man with the greying beard. I had worked that out for myself. He said he would have to bring the mower into the workshop but he was so busy that he wouldn't be able to look at it until the end of the week. I told him we were leaving then. Jan had already told me not to let the mower go away because he would speak to his mechanic friend in Le Bugue and get him to look at it. He was sure this man would be able to fix it. So that is where things are at the moment. The mower works, but not properly. As the grass is so wet I couldn't do any mowing anyway and I think I was quite lucky to cut the grass last week.

Heather and Jenny have gone to the market in Thenon. I drove past it and it really is a small and forlorn affair these days. Maybe it will improve in the summer. H. and J. say that the market was actually much better than last week. There were more stalls there and lots of people. The stall selling paella was back, as was the man selling shoes and boots, and there were two fish stalls as well. Maybe last week was a one-off because of the holiday week.

We had a lovely lunch at Anne and Michel's and they both looked well. Michel was quiet, as usual, and he let Anne taste the wine. His illness some years ago ruined his sense of smell and taste, a big problem for a wine dealer. The house was the same as usual and Anne says they are there to stay. We shall see. She would really like to go south, to the Basque country, but Michel likes Périgord and that is where their sons are now living. Michel doesn't like cities and they have lots of friends around. Brice is in Worthing, improving his English, and Florian and Terence have homes at Bars and near Hautefort. They are doing some properties up with the idea of selling them and also having gites for tourists. Anne says there just isn't any other work around here.

We had a very nice beetroot salad to start, followed by a goulash with rice and then cheese.

Wednesday, 21 April 2004

Bright and sunny. A lovely day and we deserve it, after so much rain and cold. Maybe some more people will be out looking for houses. I imagine that yesterday many of them were sitting inside, huddled around a radiator.

The hot water heater occasionally makes a noise, a buzzing sound that may be associated with a lack of water in the system, perhaps caused by an air lock. I turned the water heat down and it hasn't happened since, but it is another problem that needs to be looked at.

In the evening we went out to dinner. We tried to go to the Moulin de Mayence, but it was closed, so we went on to Archambeau in Thonac. We had the 20 euro menu and it came to 75 euros for the three, with a bottle of not very good wine. The meal was simple – soup, then a starter – mine was a salad, then magret, then cheese plus walnut oil salad, then dessert. The meal was enlivened by a French drunk, who spoke very loudly, but was not any more harm than that. He told the world he was seventy-eight and had lots of regrets.

On the way home it started to rain. There were spectacular sheets and forks of lightning and some occasional, far-off rumbles of thunder, but we missed most of it.

Thursday, 22 April 2004

The good weather has gone. It rained most of the night and was still raining in the morning. It is grey and miserable, but not cold. We may be going out today with Anne, to see her sons' homes, but that depends on whether she phones or not. If she doesn't Heather and I may go to Perigueux this afternoon. It will beat sitting here in the gloom, trying to find something to read.

Tomorrow is our last day. We have to get some presents and do a bit of shopping. I want to get some blank CDs so that I can copy some programs from the PC here and take them home. They are too big for floppy discs. I changed the mouse today. I bought one last year, but didn't fit it because the cable is short. But the old mouse was so old and kept sticking that I couldn't stand it any longer. So I changed it. It works better and by pulling the PC out from the wall a bit it will reach as far as necessary.

Afternoon, and still raining. We went to Leclerc and I bought some CD-Rs. The idea is to copy PowerPoint and PageMaker and then put them on the PC at home. But the PC would not recognise the blank CDs. We may go to Le Bugue tomorrow. I should see Gil at Wilson's and let her have information about the house. It might be useful when it comes to selling.

Friday, 23 April 2004

This morning the sun is shining and the weather forecast for the next few days is for glorious weather. At least it should be fine when we drive home tomorrow. This morning the man from Multiplaisance came to take the mower in. Jan spoke to his mechanic yesterday and he said that the problem could be anything. I though it best to get Multiplaisance to fix it because I don't want to put too much of a burden on Jan, who is very busy at the moment. The Multiplaisance man was right on time, as he always is, and promises that the mower will be ready in July when we come. I don't know how he remembers things, but he always seems to. The workshop is full of equipment, but he seems to know exactly which one belongs to which person. They haven't had time to mend the small Homelite strimmer.

In the afternoon Heather and I went to Le Bugue to give Wilson's the "Welcome to Jarripigier" file. We went for a drive around, via St Alvère, where the countryside is more open and less wooded. It was a lovely day, sunny, but with a rather chilly northwest wind. Nice in the sun, but not so good out of it. Then we came home and did some packing. There is not a lot to do and we had the usual sense of anti-climax and waiting around. Tonight Jenny said she would take us to the Soleil d'Or.

Wednesday, 7 July 2004

It is 2pm. This morning we had quite a lot of rain and it seems that more will come during the next few days. The wind is from the west, strong and blustery. This is very good news for the farmers and others here, because there has not been any serious rain for weeks and people are getting very worried. In some places watering has been banned and there are reports of rivers drying up and lakes being emptied.

We arrived on Monday, after a trouble-free journey, catching the 7.45am ferry and stopping just a few times for petrol and coffee. Then we went for dinner to the Orée du Bois. After that I telephoned M. Courcaud because the pool had not been opened. He said he had repaired the control box but could not do the pool because he could not get the keys. So he is coming this afternoon. Then the next day I went to Motoplaisance to get the mower, which had been repaired and now works well. The trouble was with the carburettor. Then I phoned Edward and Alex and we have arranged to go there on Monday.

On Tuesday we went to Thenon market, which was quite busy, and saw Roger Brière, who is going to Dax in August for three weeks of mud treatment for his hips. He is not expecting miracles, but if it helps a little it will be good. I went to see Wilson's while we were there and the lady there said that she had shown some people around on Saturday. But these days people are quite choosy. Some complained that there was dust from woodworm and that a dark patch under the bedroom window indicated that rain was getting in. They want charm, but not the idiosyncrasies that go with charm.

This morning we went to see Jan and Mary. I owe Jan 368 euros for work he has done, so I paid that. We hope to invite them over for lunch, maybe on Sunday.

We came home and did some work. Heather has been painting over the black patch in the bedroom, while I pruned the lime tree and chestnut tree outside the kitchen. Both were growing so low that they were touching the car and making everything look dark.

Thursday, 8 July 2004

Jan and Mary are coming for lunch on Sunday. They will also be coming with Jaap and Else, the Dutch couple we met last year who almost bought our house and now have a farmhouse near Fossemagne, which has lots of land and means lots of work. Jan says Jaap is not the world's greatest handyman, although he owns lots of tools. It will be nice to see them again, as we liked them very much. Sally might also come.

It rained during the night, much to everyone's relief I am sure, but this morning it was quite sunny. Now, at 10.20am, it is clouding over and looks as though it will rain again today.

M. Courcaud came yesterday to open up the pool. He and a colleague took off the cover and cleaned away much of the winter debris and then put in salt and Eau de javel. M. C. told me not to do anything – just leave it circulating, with the pump on and he will be back today. It already looks a bit cleaner. But the filter now seems to be filled up and the plastic basket is full of leaves. I imagine he will change the filter and then I shall change it again a few more times and in a day or two it will look fine. It is, however, a bit too cold for swimming.

Still, the rain has made everything look a bit greener although I am sure that they need much more than this to help the harvest. Mme Dartinset told me it was already a disaster. The fruit just hasn't had enough moisture to grow and it seems to me that the maize is much smaller this year than it was last.

Friday, 9 July 2004

The weather is much like it was yesterday – overcast, cold and looking like rain. Not the July heat we were hoping for, but no doubt everyone else is very glad. I got up at 7.30am and then went to do the pool. M. Courcaud gave me strict instructions yesterday when he was here. I had to change the filter bag last night (I did) and then again this morning, which I also did. The pool was already looking much cleaner and not so green. Yesterday M. Courcaud put in two sacks of salt and told me that after changing the filter sack this morning I had to press the switch on the machine under the pool cover (the one I burnt out last year by not screwing the wires up tightly enough) and putting the control in the cave to automatic. This means it will go on and off and not stay on all the time as it has been doing. By tomorrow it should be very clean and we have cleaned up a supply of bags in the washing machine ready for further use. M. C. says this is not really necessary but since we have the machine why not? I also asked him to look after the pool while we are away. This means it should be okay when others arrive and when we come back in August.

There is quite a lot of building work going on in Le Jarripigier. The house over the road now looks much better. The roof timbers are in place and half the tiling has been done. Directly opposite, between us and the Smiths, another house is being built, whose drive way goes down to the Montignac road. Going along the road to Thenon, two small houses have been built on the right, while a new one is going up opposite. So the village is beginning to grow again.

We went to the Périgord in Montignac last night. A good meal for 21 euros, three courses; I had confit and Heather had perch. But we both had indigestion last night and today Heather is very tired. Fortunately, we don't have very much to do, except going shopping. We need some cement for mending the corner of the pool, some tape to fix a leak in the loo, some earth for the container by the drive and some plants as well – geraniums should be okay. Tonight we shall eat in.

Saturday, 10 July 2004

The meal last night was a disaster. We had a pizza-style frozen meal, which only needed to be heated up, but the oven was too hot and it came out burnt to a crisp. So we had pasta with tuna instead. Tonight we are eating out.

It is another mixed day. Cloudy, with some bright spells, which are very warm, but not much rain so far, although it looks as though that will arrive at any minute. We read, fixed a leak on the downstairs loo and then hoovered the swimming pool, which looks quite clean but cloudy – this could be the salt which has not fully dissolved. Still, it has come along very well I think.

Monday, 12 July 2004

Another dull, cold grey day. Where is the heatwave of last year? We are going to see Alex and Edward at Brâ today. It will take about two hours to get there and we shall take camera and art things, but as it is raining at the moment we probably won't do very much. On the way we have to stop to get a top step for the pool steps and some more Round Up.

Yesterday we had Jan and Mary and Jaap and Else to lunch – roast lamb with roast potatoes. It was very nice. The whole thing lasted all afternoon and we ate out by the pool, about the first time we have been able to do that all week. Jaap and Else have taken possession of their new house and said they sometimes regret not buying ours. There is a lot of work to be done there it seems.

The Smiths are arriving tomorrow, or possibly today, so we might get to see them very briefly.

Tuesday, 13 July 2004

The Smiths did arrive and came to see us in the evening. Today is our last day. This morning we went to Les Eyzies to an exhibition of art works – souvenirs etc. – and bought some bird-song whistles and some pâté as presents. Ella, Jan and Mary's daughter, was working there for the summer. Pretty boring and badly paid. She is at Bordeaux University, studying film editing, but she says it is boring, because the teachers aren't very good. If they were better, they would no doubt be editing films instead of talking about it. We tried to get a key cut at Le Bugue market, but it was so busy, being market day, that we gave up and went to Perigueux instead. There is a place at Leclerc that does it. We planned to go to lunch at Bars but in the end decided we would eat at home and then go out this evening. This afternoon I mowed the lawn – five complete loads, although the grass looked quite short. Then I drove up and did Douglas's lawn as well. They were still out at lunch.

Thursday, 19 August 2004

We caught the 7.45am ferry from Dover, but instead of coming straight down, via Paris, we went to the Burgundy district and stayed the night at the Hotel de la Poste in Beaune. It is a very nice hotel, expensive (about 330 euros, including breakfast, dinner and garage) but we liked it. Beaune itself is lovely, a small historic town surrounded by an ancient wall and a *peripherique* around that (the hotel is on that road). We got there at about 4pm and that gave us time to go for a walk round the town, admiring the old buildings and the elaborate roofs. We thought that Burgundy would be a good place to visit one day – it would make an excellent base for a short holiday. The next morning we set off, driving through rolling hills covered with vineyards and villages with famous names. We drove alongside a canal for a long way and thought that would be a good way to travel.

As we went further south, the weather began to change, along with the scenery. Goodbye vines and goodbye sun. It began to rain. By the time we reached Vichy and the motorway it was pouring. We continued on our way, past Clermont-Ferrand, making for Aurillac, where we planned to stay. The rain was now torrential, so that driving was quite difficult. Then we got off the motorway and drove along a twisting N road towards Aurillac. Unfortunately, Aurillac was having some sort of festival. Lots of roads were closed off and the traffic was heavy, so we gave up the idea of staying there and decided to go straight to Le Jarripigier.

We got there between 6.30pm and 7pm, and found that the storm had beaten us to it. Water had come into the kitchen, down the light fittings and had also poured into the cave and the downstairs bedroom. According to the *Sud-Ouest*, Thenon had something like 4 inches of rain in thirty minutes. Bars was even worse. They were hit by hail, which destroyed the tiles of thirty to fifty houses. One man said it was raining just as hard in his living room as it was outside.

We spent much of Wednesday trying to clean up. It was sunny in the morning and we thought the worst was over. It was, but there was still something left, because in the afternoon it began to rain and was soon dripping into the kitchen again. The gutter facing the pool was blocked (this happened once before) but we managed to clear that and the rain stopped coming in. But the gutter on the road side was also blocked and the rain was still coming in from there. We used the long broom from the swimming pool and managed to clear it. The rain stopped and so did the dripping. But we still don't know if we have solved the problem. We made a channel round the cave door and cleared out the water inside. Another problem is cooking. We are not sure about using the light over the kitchen, or even the cooker. So last night we bought some microwave food and used that.

We slept downstairs, because we thought it would be too warm upstairs. It turned out to be quite cold, with only a blanket, so tonight we plan to move upstairs.

The good news is that the hot water works a treat and the pool is looking very clean. It was filled right up when we arrived so I pumped out about 4 inches of water to get it back to the right level. The temperature is about 26 degrees.

The other inconvenience is that the telephone was not working. I phoned France Telecom who checked and said there was nothing wrong with the line. So this morning we went to Leclerc and bought a new one, which works perfectly.

Friday, 20 August 2004

Because the water was still getting into the kitchen – coming down the light – we went to La Roseraie for dinner. It was good, and we slept well. But in the morning Heather found that the light fitting was still wet. Although it rained a little during the night there was no sign that fresh water had got in, so I think the dampness came from water that had already accumulated. Nevertheless, it was worrying and so I phoned up some roofers to see if they could come and look at it. We need to get the roof checked for leaks, because the kitchen ceiling is marked and there is no saying when the next bad storm will come. The man who answered said somebody would come during the day, but of course at this time of the year lots of people are on holiday – Renomat is closed, for example – and others are occupied with Bars, which has more problems than we do. So there is not much to do here but wait. And hope it doesn't rain. Or, if it does, that it doesn't get into the house.

Saturday, 21 August 2004

A dry day so far, although it is getting cloudy this afternoon. Last night I phoned M. Daubisse, who did some work here when Mel was around, and he said he will come to look at the roof tomorrow lunchtime. That is a considerable relief.

We went though Bars this morning. Scenes of devastation as a result of the storm and the hail. Many buildings have tarpaulins over them and some buildings seem to have been destroyed almost – one tower was full of huge holes, and there were trees down everywhere, probably because of the wind rather than the hail. The ground must have been so sodden that the trees could not grip. Other trees were split in half or had branches torn off.

We had lunch by the pool – a potato soup, made by Heather, followed by pâté, cheese etc. Tonight we think we might go out for a meal.

Sunday, 22 August 2004

The storms seem to have stopped. Yesterday was fine and dry and today at 8.30am the sun is shining and it promises to be a perfect day. The water has stopped seeping into the kitchen and M.

Daubisse has promised to come at lunchtime to have a look at the roof. We went to Sergeac and saw the Deljarrys. Claude and Madame were both well, but Madame, who said she is ninety-four, was much older than the last time we saw them. She is quite deaf and seems forgetful about things.

The mushroom season started on Monday. The paper is full of reports about cêpes, which sell for 10 to 15 euros a kilo; Claude said there were none around Sergeac but there were lots around Valajoulx. We didn't find any in our wood, just some rather ancient unpleasant yellow-brown things that looked very unappetising.

Tuesday, 24 August 2004

There was a small storm last night. One enormous bang overhead at 3am, but most of the spectacle took place elsewhere. It rained during the night, but nothing got in. This morning we went to Shopi to get bread and the paper because it is market day and the town will be closed. Also, the baker at the bottom is closed.

Mary phoned last night to ask about the house. She might be able to find a buyer and I said we would let her have the 7% that Wilson's will charge. No word yet (it is now 10.15am). We bought some paint and brushes yesterday and today hope to start work on the second bedroom and then the kitchen, which we are leaving so that it can dry out completely.

There were people mushrooming everywhere yesterday and the papers have lots of news about the season starting. The rain has brought the mushrooms out, but although we found quite a lot around us, we don't know if they are good or not.

Wednesday, 25 August 2004

Today, at 12.15pm, it has started to drizzle. But that was forecast and anyway, we have both been busy indoors. Heather has been painting the ground-floor bedroom, while I have been cleaning out the utility room. What a lot of junk, all piled up, taking advantage of the fact that there is lots of space. I also cleaned off lots of cobwebs. Will do more soon. The trouble with having lots of room is that you fill it, because you don't put things away carefully.

Yesterday was interesting. The weather was good and we sat around and read. Then Mary came round and told us that Cass

Hamilton had some friends staying who might be interested in the house. While she was with us Cass phoned to say that the people were there and could they come round? So I said yes and they came. They are a very pleasant couple from Cornwall, where they say the people are very unfriendly and it takes forty years to be accepted. They don't want to wait that long and are planning to settle in France. Their names are Tam and Paula. They liked the house, but are going to Aix en Provence at the weekend and so there wont be much happening for a while, even if they want to buy. If they do, Mary will get the commission and said she can look after the notaire and all the legalities. That will be useful.

Today I had a call from someone called Vincent from IMOL a property firm. Anne Trouvé had told him we were interested in selling. I think he wanted us to take out an advert, but I said we were already dealing with an agent, so we weren't in the market at the moment. I gave him details of the house and so we shall see if anything comes of that. I phoned Anne and left a message but I think they must be away for the summer.

All in all, quite productive. Mary said that September is a good buying time, presumably because people have spent the summer looking round and now want to choose something. I learned two useful things today. The French version of 1471 is 3131 and the number for directory enquiries is 12. We have to go to Perigueux to get a new *annuaire*. Ours is two years old.

Thursday, 26 August 2004

The forecast is for sunshine and showers, but it is still not very warm. I had a call at about 9am from a woman who had received a call from our number yesterday. What happened was that when we got back from the Moulin de Mayence, where we had a lovely meal, I pressed 3131 and there was a number on the answering service. I pressed 5, but there was no answer, although the phone rang. This morning she must have done the same because she phoned and said: "Did you phone me last night?" and then she asked "Who are you?" Obviously there was some sort of mix up. Anyway, we had a friendly chat – she knew Le Jarripigier because her sister lived next door to M. Barbini. She said we should go and get some mushrooms, because they are absolutely delicious now. I said we were scared. Yesterday Mary said that she was poisoned by a mushroom some time ago. It made her sick and ill and she was glad she did not eat it all.

Today I swept up the pool a bit. It is very clean, but there are still a few leaves floating around. I tried to chop up some wood for the winter, but the mallet broke. I will have to get a new one.

Saturday, 28 August 2004

Mima phoned yesterday to say she probably won't be able to come. She has a bad neck and it has flared up again. She doesn't want to be away from medical help (she is thinking of trying acupuncture) and thinks the journey might be too much for her. That will be a great shame, but I am sure she is doing the right thing. We got the mallet and other things yesterday and today hope to do useful things about the house, although Heather isn't feeling too good, as she has bad indigestion. The weather is cold. Cloudy, no rain, but certainly cold in the morning. We both wear sweaters. When I went to get the paper just after 8am the temperature outside was 13 degrees.

Sunday, 29 August 2004

Cloudy, not very warm, some rain this morning. The rest of the week is supposed to be good. We hope so. We had lunch in – roast turkey, with vegetables. Quite nice. This afternoon I walked down the road past the new houses on the right and the little wooden house being built on the left. Then I turned left and walked down past the three houses that lie down the path and on to the field below. Then back up through the field to the main road. I phoned Viv and Mum this afternoon. All seems well. They went to the Yalding Organic Garden today. I filled in some of the cracks in the kitchen wall this morning but felt too tired to do much more. Wine at lunchtime is the reason. But it looks quite a lot better. I will finish it tomorrow and then we shall paint it.

It feels very autumnal now. Even if the good weather does come back, the days are now shorter and we shall have to get Desjoyaux to close down the pool for the winter very shortly. Heather went in once. But I only got as far as my knees. Very cold (about 25 degrees).

Tuesday, 31 August 2004

It is 10.15am. The sky to the east is blue and the sun is rising high. There are a few clouds away to the south, but nothing to worry about. The forecast is for more tomorrow. At last, summer.

We are going to see Jaap and Else for lunch. We found their house yesterday, not far from Fossemagne. Yesterday we went to Brantôme and had lunch at a very nice restaurant called Au Fil de l'Eau. Brantôme is a very pretty town, with an ancient abbey and a river running through the middle. But it was a fairly dull, cloudy day. We did a bit of work on the kitchen in the morning, patching up the cracks with mastic. It looks much better now, and tomorrow we plan to paint it. I did some repair work on the step outside the living room, but the cement is too white. I shall get some grey this afternoon and smooth that over, it won't be so noticeable.

Wednesday, 1 September 2004

At last, a perfect day. Blue sky, sunshine, no clouds, but still a bit chilly, with a slight wind from the north. Heather had a swim, but I didn't. We spent the morning painting the kitchen. It looks so much better now, even though I don't think Ernie would rate our work very highly. The marks left by the storm have gone and it should look more attractive to potential buyers.

We had lunch with Jaap and Else. Very nice it was too. Their house is in need of a lot of work, but the potential is certainly there. I don't think they plan to do too much themselves, but they will get others to do it for them. In some cases this means new beams and floors. There are some outbuildings too that all have potential. They plan to live there permanently. I wish them well. But I'm glad it's not me.

This afternoon was mostly reading. I am reading Roy Jenkins' biography of Churchill, which I am enjoying very much. Other books this holiday have included *The Court of the Red Tsar* by Simon Sebag-Montefiore, a chilling account of life in the Kremlin and Russia during Stalin's time. What a monster. Also Ruth Rendell's *The Rottweiler* and a good thriller called *Want to Play?* by an American woman writer, P.J. Tracy. I also managed to finish *Life and Fate* by Vasily Grossman.

Thursday, 2 September 2004

It is now 9.50am. Last night it rained quite a lot and there was some distant thunder, but the house is fine. This morning the sky started off bright, but clouds have started to develop and it might rain again. But the promise for the next few days is sunshine, sunshine, which will be fine for us when we are painting. I went to the Shopi to get the paper and bread, but there are roadworks on the N89, outside the post office, with single-file traffic. Schools have started again today and there were lots of mothers outside the nursery school by the Shopi. In town, the hardware shop by the newsagent was open – it closed last year – and some men were working inside, getting it ready for some new enterprise. It will be interesting to see what happens to it. It was all so exciting I forgot to post a card to Jenny and had to go back to town to do so.

Yesterday afternoon I mowed the lawn. The mower works perfectly since being serviced in July. I scattered the grass cuttings below the hazel, filling up holes and trying to provide compost. Today I have to phone Desjoyaux and see about the hivernage. There are a few things more to do, but by and large all is done. On Sunday we go off to Brâ.

Friday, 3 September 2004

A glorious day, sunny and warm – the best so far. Yesterday, which was also good, we went to Sarrazac to have lunch with Anne. Michel wasn't there – he had to go to Bordeaux on business – but another friend called Michel was. He and Anne are going to walk to Compostela very shortly. After lunch, we went off to see the house near Hautefort owned by their sons. Brice was there, now a tall, slim young man, very nice and friendly. He has spent a few months in England to learn the language. Liked Brighton but didn't think much of Galway, where the people were very unfriendly.

Today we did very little except sit by the pool and read. I cleaned out the cave and cemented the steps from the living room – they should be a bit safer now. We thought about going out but the heat and lethargy were too much, so we didn't. Last evening two men came to the house, to have a look, both local, probably father and son. They had heard the house was for sale and thought they would have a look. I think they were rather surprised to find us there, but I didn't mind. I showed them around and said that if they wanted another look they should get in touch with Wilson's. I told Wilson's this morning.

Monday, 13 September 2004

We are now back home. The last week was spent at Brâ on our painting holiday. The tutor was Tom Coates. We both thought that it was hard work. Tom has great energy and thought that any minute not spent painting was wasted. We both found it rather tiring and the standard was very high. Some of the painters were very good and they all tended to paint in the Tom Coates style. We began to feel more at home after a few days and certainly I felt that we had learned a lot. He paints mostly in oils – that inspired us to take up oils ourselves – and mostly painted using very small boards. Most of the others were the same. His pictures tended to be quite dark, with the emphasis on texture rather than colour, and he built up blocks rather than concentrating on line. He does not draw with a pencil but uses his brush. The first outline is often in oil diluted with turps.

On the first day we went to Argentat, further up the Dordogne, a very pretty town on the river. We painted there in the morning and had a picnic lunch. I thought my watercolour was terrible and Heather was disappointed with hers, although I thought it was good: the trouble was we compared our efforts to Tom's and the other people's. We went to Bretonnoux the next day and painted by the river and in the market: lots of drawings and sketching. I was trying to be much freer and less meticulous.

We did some painting in Beaulieu – it really is a pretty town, with a market, two lovely churches and a river setting. Nice shops as well.

Monday, 25 October 2004

We came down yesterday, having caught the 7.45 ferry from Dover. It was a very pleasant journey. The weather was fine and traffic was light, although there were a few jams around Paris, mostly caused by roadworks. We got here at about ten past six (French time) and would have got here earlier but Lanouaille was blocked by a vide-grenier and we were sent on a deviation. Our fault, in a way, for deciding to go via St Yrieix rather than Brive.

Today was a chores day. This involved:

a) Phoning Wilson's to discuss the price. We have dropped it to 205,000. They said there had been a lot of interest but no one had come back with an offer. Maybe the price drop will stimulate interest.

b) Phoning M. Daubisse about the roof. He was there and I said I would send him our address. We want him to clean off the moss and replace any missing or broken tiles. He can then send the estimate to us in England.

c) Putting a sill on the bottom of the cave door. This should stop any rain splashes from getting in.

d) Blocking a mouse hole that has suddenly appeared by the kitchen door. I filled it with wire wool and then put some plaster over it.

All these jobs were done early, so we went to Bassillac to do some shopping. The art shop was shut but we got some food etc. at the supermarket there.

Last night we went to eat in Montignac. The Périgord by the river was open and we went there, but it had changed its name and seemed more inviting. The food was very good and the service excellent. Tomorrow we have to go to Sarlat to about a new Carte Bleue.

This afternoon we went for a spin – through St Leon and Peyzac le Moustier, then left past the Chateau de Peuch to Fleurac and then via lots of twisting roads that we didn't know, via Manaurie to le Bugue and then back through Rouffignac, where major works have taken place on the village square. A new surface laid down and some spaces left for planting new trees.

Wednesday, 27 October 2004

Yesterday we went to Sarlat and got the new card and new cheque book. Both were waiting there, although I had asked for them to be sent. It seems that they like you to go to the bank and sign for them there, which I did. Then we had a coffee and went to Thenon, where we signed the new mandate lowering the price to 205,000 euros. We also saw the Brières, who talked about retirement. About three more years, Roger reckons, and then they will leave Thenon and hope to move to Bearn, further south. The Basque country is out of the question – it is much too expensive there – but they want to leave Thenon. It is dying, there is nothing to do and it is generally too boring. I must say that I sympathise.

Strangely, on Monday evening we had a visit from a prospective purchaser, an English lady who had driven up from Morocco. We hope the new price will attract offers as well as interest. In Sarlat we managed to park on the Traverse, down the road from the bank, and thought we were very clever. But we also got a parking ticket (11 euros) because we didn't know it is now a *payant* zone.

Then we went to Perigueux and had lunch and after that went to the art shop at Bassillac, looking for a *pochade* (combined easel and paintbox) without success. And then home. Quite a busy day really.

This morning it is overcast and quite chilly. The whole feeling now is very autumnal, although in fact we have had very good weather, despite the abysmal forecasts. We think we will go home tomorrow, stopping en route and then going via Hesdin to get some wine from the Wine Society shop there. We shall take some things back with us – books, tools etc. There is no point leaving them here.

This morning we went out for a drive. We went through Les Eyzies and St Cyprien and then across the river and on to Monpazier. The weather was dull, but at least it wasn't raining and it was perfect for driving around, because there was very little traffic and the visibility was very good. Nothing much was open. We looked for a bar in Monpazier but everything seemed to have closed down now that the season is over. On the way back we went through Beaumont, another *bastide*, which was a little more lively, but we didn't stop, and came home via Le Bugue and Rouffignac. Tonight we go to see Jan and Mary.

* * *

Friday, 25 March 2005
It is 11.10am. A bright, sunny, lovely day. The birds are singing, including the cuckoo and the garden looks lovely. Jan came along a few weeks ago and cleared away lots of rubbish and dead wood – some trees had come down in storms. We had a fun trip down. The

French seamen were on strike a few days ago and the M20 was blocked by lorries in Operation Stack. We were worried that we would not be able to leave on Thursday morning, as planned, but P&O said their ships were operating, so we took a chance and left early, intending to catch the 9.15am sailing. But there was very little traffic and because we used the M2 we missed the lorries. When we got to Dover the port was quieter than ever. We thought that lots of people must have cancelled their trips. Anyway, we were so early that we made the 8.15 sailing. All went well after that, although there was a thirty minute delay at Calais because of tbe strike. But the big hold-up came getting around Paris. It took two hours. Sometimes we have done it in forty minutes.

One highlight came after we passed Limoges. The sky darkened and it became clear that we were passing through the edge of a storm. There were flashes of lightning, then rain, and then a series of rainbows – we counted three. They were so bright and intense against the dark sky that we could identify the various colours quite easily (Richard of York Gave Battle in Vain). We got to Thenon at 7.45pm and decided to eat at the Orée du Bois, before coming to the house. While we were there we met the Smiths, with Janie, and had a pleasant meal with them.

We got to the house at about 11pm and found that all was well except for a leak in one of the upstairs pipes. Not a major problem, but it obviously needed fixing. We tried putting tape around it, but it was no good and so I phoned Jan and Mary. Mary very kindly contacted a plumber called Jean-Michel, who is a friend of theirs, and he came at about 10.30am. He fixed it in about five minutes, including a tap in the bathroom that didn't work properly. He charged 20 euros so I gave him 25.

That set our minds at rest and we feel we can now get on with enjoying ourselves. Our plumbing problem, incidentally, was as nothing compared with some other people Jan and Mary know. They had a burst pipe in the attic and they arrived to find the house flooded. There are problems over insurance, apparently. So our leak seems very small. But even so, these are the things that happen when you have a holiday home that is empty all winter. Apparently thetemperature dropped to –15 at one point. But now it seems just like spring.

In the afternoon we sat in the garden and read and dozed. I did some lawn mowing, but the mower was not working well and in the end packed up. I shall have to get it serviced. Fortunately, the Motoplaisance place on the N89 still seems to be open.

Saturday, 26 March 2005

We went to Multiplaisance early this morning and the mechanic will come on Tuesday morning to collect the mower. Another glorious day and the local paper says that there are already fears of a drought later in the year if it doesn't rain more. There is enough water in the big rivers, thanks to the snow in the mountains, but the farmers are already getting short.

Sunday, 27 March 2005

Today we went to the restaurant Aux Berges de la Vézère, which used to be the Périgord, in Montignac, with Douglas, Shirley and Janie. We had a very good 25 euro menu. I started with salmon in a cream and walnut sauce, followed by magret. The chef came round and said hullo and I think it was his wife who served. The other waitress was a lady who had been at the restaurant when they took it over last year. The restaurant has been smartened up a bit and was very comfortable, although not full.

It has rained most of the day. Good news for the farmers but not for us. Still, they need it more than we do. M. Dartinset saw us yesterday. He will be eighty in October. His wife has problems with arthritis. I told him about acupuncture. Apparently Sylvie came round with some dogs, but she is living in Perigueux. Jenny has fallen in love with a golden Labrador, but he is mostly interested in other dogs at present.

Monday, 28 March 2005

Cloudy, some rain, lots during the night; but that is probably what is needed here. In the morning we met a New Zealand couple who are staying at the house that is sliding down the hill. They are from Wellington and are visiting their family. Then we went to get some shopping and on the way back stopped to see Jan and Mary. Ella was there as well. Their gite is coming along very well and I paid Mary some money that I owed her for showing people around, getting the plumber and so on. It is really very good having such people to keep and eye on the place. Now it is 1.30pm and we shall have some lunch soon. It is none too warm, either in the house or outside, but we have turned the heating up and it should be warm enough soon. It is very quiet outside and the birds are singing as I write this. And the whole of the summer is to come.

Wednesday, 30 March 2005

It is 11.15am. Today the weather is wet and unpromising. But at least it is quite warm. We think we may have an air lock in the heating and water, because every so often there is a noise when the heating comes on. It is more annoying than anything, but if we sell the house soon it doesn't really matter. Some people came round yesterday (French), and more are coming on Friday morning. I shall give the spare keys to Vicky, which will save her from having to go to Mary every time someone calls. We went to Jardiland yesterday and bought some plants for the old cistern head by the driveway entrance and some shrubs to plant on the bank behind the wood store. The new house next door is nearing completion and it looks hideous – completely the wrong style for the area. Worse, it does rather overlook our property, so we think the shrubs will help to screen it and give us some privacy. Tomorrow we hope to go to Millau to look at the bridge. The weather forecast is better for the end of the week, so it should be a pleasant day out. On Friday we are going to La Commanderie for dinner with the Smiths, who are leaving for home the day after. The rain is now coming down harder than ever. A long way to go to read a book.

Friday, 1 April 2005

Yesterday was a highlight. We went on a day trip to look at the new bridge at Millau, which opened last year and connects the two sections of the A75 motorway. It cost 3.90 euros to cross, but it was well worth it. What a fabulous piece of design and engineering. There are seven huge pillars, the largest being higher than the Eiffel tower, and it is 2.5km long. We bought some photos, because it is very difficult to take anything with my camera that will do justice to it. To build the bridge they installed a huge machine at each end and then pushed the roadway out to connect with the other end. I shall have to get more information about it, perhaps on the Internet, because they didn't have very much there apart from photos and a short film. The whole journey was 385 miles. It would have been more enjoyable if the weather had been kinder, but it was quite good really. Heather felt quite ill in the morning – cold, tired and hungry - but recovered after lunch.

I would like to know more about the Massif Central. I left my Michelin guide at home. It is a mixture of granite and volcanic rock with lots of limestone around Gramat in the southwest. There is very little arable farming, maybe because the soil is not good enough, and it is also quite high. The fields are small and often surrounded by crumbling stone walls, no doubt collected from the fields themselves. There are lots of sheep around, a long-legged variety, some of them black. The milk goes to make Roquefort cheese.

Saturday, 2 April 2005

It is a very blustery day so far, but at least it is not raining. Yesterday evening we went to La Commanderie with the Smiths. It was quite a pleasant meal (32 and 25 euros) but rather disappointing on the whole. Douglas's meat was too well done, but mine was quite good. We are hoping to go to Fanlac tomorrow for lunch. I went to the Multiplaisance place, but they have not fixed the mower. It needs to be taken apart and the motor properly serviced. This could be quite a long job, because the whole machine has to be stripped down. So I have to go back on Tuesday to see what they say. I telephoned Jan this morning to see if he can mow the lawn in the meantime. He said he would come in next week. Heather and Jen have just been to the Shopi to get some food.

It is now 5.30pm. Heather and I went to Couze, near Lalinde, this afternoon to look at a paper museum recommended by Douglas and Shirley. It was a lovely drive, through Le Bugue and the Cingle de Tremolat, but when we arrived we found it was closed on Saturdays. Never mind, we intend to go next week. On the way back we got held up by a cycle race. I don't think it was a major event, but it was quite good fun. Four cyclists led, then a group of about twelve, then a few groups of three or four and then a larger group of about twenty, with stragglers after that. We joined on the end when we were allowed to but then got deviated and lost. But we found ourselves again, without too much trouble, and came back Les Eyzies.

Tomorrow we shall eat at Fanlac.

Sunday, 3 April 2005

We had lunch at Le Croquant and enjoyed it. Heather had the vegetarian menu and Jenny and I had the traditional. Both cost 18 euros. We had a bottle of Tiregand with it. There was plenty of food, indeed, by the end of the meal we were all full. Heather's meal starred an omelette. I'm not sure if this qualifies as vegetarian, but she liked it so it didn't really matter. The forecast is for rain today, but so far we haven't had any. Although it is cloudy and not very warm. Next week should be better.

Monday, 4 April 2005

So far, so good. There are a few lacy clouds, very high in the sky, and there is a little wind. But the sun is shining as I write (it is 9.30am) and this afternoon we hope to go to the paper museum at Couze, which was closed on Saturday. Yesterday afternoon we just sat around, too lethargic to do anything after our meal. I did some painting, enough to see how bad I am but also learning a little on the way. It really is a very engrossing hobby and I am glad we both enjoy it.

Tuesday, 5 April 2005

Another damp day. We went to the market this morning. It was a little busier than last week and the fish stall was there. We bought some plants and on the way back went to Multiplaisance to see about the mower. The man said that he managed to get it started, but it still needs work done, which will involve taking it apart. He hopes to have it ready by Friday, after I told him we were leaving on Saturday. We are going to Bars for lunch. It looks quite good and Jan and Mary recommended it.

Now back from lunch. The Relais Gourmand is very good. The man who does the cooking also did the serving today. We began with vegetable soup, which was very nice; quite clear liquid, with lots of vegetables in it and the whole thing was very tasty. Then came a quiche followed by pork with beans – delicious. Then cheese and, finally, apple with a caramel sauce. It was lovely. The total cost for three, including wine, was 34.50 euros.

Some people came to look at the house in the afternoon, from Wales, I believe. We have had at least five sets of visitors so far and although no one has made an offer yet, the number of prospective purchasers is very encouraging.

Wednesday, 6 April 2005

The excitement this morning was a mouse in Jenny's room. It meant she could not get up until it was light. We think it might be trapped behind the wardrobe. I have put a gumboot there, with some cheese in it, and have turned on the rodent repeller. If that doesn't work we shall have to move the wardrobe. While this was going a man from Total Gaz rang to say that he wanted to come to fix a small gas leak reported by the man who carried out the inspection last week. It is very small, but needs to be done. He duly arrived, but could not fix the leak and will come back on Friday morning, between 8.30am and 9am.

A French couple came round this afternoon and seemed very interested. I gave them our name and address but didn't take theirs. Silly. We went to Bassillac to get some CDs, but the computer won't recognise them. I don't know why.

Thursday, 7 April 2005

We went to Brâ today to have lunch with Edward and Alex. A lovely day, and the drive over was pleasant, despite the fact that it rained all the time. We had a look round Alex's studio on the top floor. There must have been about thirty or forty oils there, in various stages of completion. I think this is a good way to work. Keep things and go back to them until you are satisfied and don't try to do it all in one go. You have to be able to step back and think. It is sixty-one miles there from here.

Friday, 8 April 2005

The Total Gaz man is here. He has a trailer with a huge tank on it, into which he is emptying our gas cylinder. When it is empty he will be able to repair the leak, and will then put the gas back into it. It will mean our gas will be turned off for about an hour. Tonight Jan and Mary are coming over for an aperitif before going out with friends. We will go to the Soleil d'Or for our last meal. It is a lovely day, but rather on the chilly side. We are beginning to pack our things up.

Sunday, 3 July 2005

Here we are on what should be our last holiday. Tomorrow Gil Kendall, the estate agent, is coming with documents for us to sign, which will mean the house being sold to a Dutch lady teacher. She has already signed and after this everything will go to the notaire, Maitre Labaisse, for action. There are no problems apparently, as the buyer has cash and seems quite keen to buy.

The weather today, like yesterday, is perfect. Not a cloud in the sky, hot, clear. The house is looking good. The garden is a bit overgrown but okay and the pool is clear and shining. There was a lot of dirt on the bottom but the water was fine. I put the pump on only to discover that it didn't work. So I phoned M. Courcaud and left a message on his answer phone. About ten minutes later he arrived (this was yesterday afternoon). He had been doing jobs around the house and didn't hear the phone ring, but his wife did and she gave him the message: "M. Kohn has a breakdown!" M. C. got in his van and came straight round. I wasn't really expecting him until Monday, so top marks for service. He fixed the problem in about ten minutes and the pump works perfectly. The dirt is clearing up and I went for a swim yesterday afternoon. The water temperate was 80 degrees F.

We came down via Burgundy and stayed overnight at Auxerre. The hotel was by the river and we ate at a restaurant just up the road called Le Bounty. A lovely town on the Yonne. The old town is on the central hill, which is topped by a cathedral, which is no doubt worth a visit. Auxerre is one of those towns that deserves to be seen more closely, perhaps worth a night or two, like Beaune and Bourges. We arrived here about 2.30pm and went out and got some shopping and made a few phone calls and settled down. We ate at the Berges de la Vézère last night. Nice, but perhaps not as good as usual. Even so, sitting outside by the river was perfect.

Monday, 4 July 2005

Yesterday was very hot and sunny. Not a cloud in the sky until the afternoon and then it became a bit grey, just as the forecast said. We had intended to go out for a meal at lunchtime, but it was so hot and we had food in the house, so we stayed at home. Jan came round in the morning and he and Mary came in the evening. We will go out to Maria's this evening. It will be a change, as we haven't been for some years. They say it is very good still.

Heather's hand hurts this morning. It just needs a twinge or so to set it off and then it aches the next morning. I think it just needs to be strapped up better, because it is very difficult not to jar it.

Today the weather has changed completely. It is cloudy and last night there was a thunderstorm. But it was never overhead, about five miles away at the closest. It rained but not very much and the forecast is for much of the same during the next few days. It is now 11.30am and the sun is trying to come through. The temperature has dropped right down into the twenties.

Gil Kendall arrived just after 2pm and we then set about signing lots of documents. These included the *Vente d'Immeuble*, the *synthese des diagnostics* – this is really a check carried out to see if the house had termites (no), lead (no) or asbestos (possibly in some floor tiles and the roof of the shed); the *plan parcellaire*, and various other bits of paper, which are of more interest to the buyer than us. It is quite a business selling a house in France. Anyway, everything seems to be going well and the whole thing should be completed by 30 September. Gil would like us to come down just before that to sign everything at the notaire's, although, we could do it by mail from England if necessary. We will try to come down. Gil also said that she will deal with the water board etc. and let them know about the change of ownership. We only have to let the phone people know – we also have to tell them that their phone (rented) went wrong so we threw it away and bought one.

Heather spoke to Vicky at Lafayette, who asked us to let her know in writing that we have sold and let her know to whom. I'll do that, but won't give her the address of the buyer.

Gil took some of our books and told us that there is an English library in Le Bugue, so that is somewhere for us to dump a lot of our books. We can take them to Gil and she will get them to the library.

Apparently the property market has slowed right down here as well. Wilson's have sold six houses to Dutch buyers so far this year, compared with only three for the whole of last year, but the English are not buying. They all want cheap houses, and then are disappointed at what they are going to get.

Tuesday, 5 July 2005

I went to Multiplaisance this morning. The mower is okay, apart from some relatively minor problems with the seat, and it will be brought back at about 2.30 this afternoon. After that we shall go over to see Jan and Mary's new gite, which they are living in while a Danish family have their house – all ten of them. We ate at Maria's last night. Excellent meal for 18 euros each. The total bill for four including wine, was 80 euros. No sign of Isabelle, but the food and service were excellent. Maria seems to do it all. The restaurant was not very busy, but it was a Monday night. Apparently they do not open on Saturdays. Another lovely day, despite the forecasts.

Tuesday, 4 October 2005

Well, it is nearly all over. We have signed the house away to a Dutch school teacher, who seems very pleasant so we don't mind so much and we hope she enjoys it as much as we did. They came to the house in the afternoon on Friday and we showed the buyer and her partner around, showing them where the various control panels were and so on. During the week we had taken away the furniture, some of which will go to Jan and May and some of which will be sold.

After the tour we all went off to Fossemagne to see the notaire for the signing. It took a long time, because she had to explain all the legal formalities and make sure we understood and agreed. Christopher Kendall and a colleague came as well to help out. I had to pay capital gains tax of 270.40 euros, which was worked out by the *representatif fiscale.* He charged 1,973 euros for the service. I also had to pay 506 euros for a termite check. This is a legal requirement. If anything had been found I would have had to pay for it to be attended to, but there was nothing – just some asbestos on the roof of the garden shed, which was not a problem. By 7pm it was all over. We shook hands and all went our separate ways.

Our overwhelming feeling was relief. The dream had begun to turn sour and we had started to resent having to dash down to the Dordogne every time we had a few days available. And I was tired of paying bills and arranging for repairs and maintenance. I arranged for the phone to be cut off and stopped the monthly payments for the *taxes d'habitation* and *foncières.* The sheer running costs of a house in France are high, so not having to pay them will be a gain.

On the last day we took Jan and Mary and Ella and Sally to the Bistro Gourmand at Bars. It is a really excellent restaurant with good food and a very warm welcome. It is a perfect place for our last meal as French property owners.

Notes

1. A garden centre near Perigueux.

2. A restaurant on the N89 near Thenon.

3. Mel McHugh was an Englishman who lived in the area at the time and did quite a lot of work for us.

4. We had changed the pool from a chemical-based system to one that relied mainly on salt for cleanliness. It turned out to be a good investment, especially if the pool has had to be left for a long period of time.

5. A restaurant in Thenon.

6. One of my colleagues.

7. The previous owner of our house.

8. The local daily newspaper.

9. My cousins, who were staying at Sergeac.

10. A chain of DIY stores. Much like B&Q.

11. Our neighbour.

12. A garden shed where we kept various tools.

13 A friend from home, who was looking after our house and cats while we were away

14. A colleague from the office, now retired.

15. Friends from home.

16. Jan Zewucki, a friend who lives at Plazac.

17. A friend from home, who stayed at our house in the summer.

18 My younger sister.

19. Friends.

20. My American nephew and his wife.

21. My sister Vivien was moving home at this time.

22. A credit card from the Banque Nationale de Paris. Quite useful, as it is a Visa card. Many places in France do not accept MasterCard.

23. A friend who used to live in Bordeaux, but has since moved to the Dordogne.